"The Object Lessons series achieves something very close to magic: the books take ordinary—even banal—objects and animate them with a rich history of invention, political struggle, science, and popular mythology. Filled with fascinating details and conveyed in sharp, accessible prose, the books make the everyday world come to life. Be warned: once you've read a few of these, you'll start walking around your house, picking up random objects, and musing aloud: 'I wonder what the story is behind this thing?'"

Steven Johnson, author of *Where Good Ideas Come From* and *How We Got to Now*

"Object Lessons describes themselves as 'short, beautiful books,' and to that, I'll say, amen. . . . If you read enough Object Lessons books, you'll fill your head with plenty of trivia to amaze and annoy your friends and loved ones—caution recommended on pontificating on the objects surrounding you. More importantly, though . . . they inspire us to take a second look at parts of the everyday that we've taken for granted. These are not so much lessons about the objects themselves, but opportunities for self-reflection and storytelling. They remind us that we are surrounded by a wondrous world, as long as we care to look."

John Warner, *The Chicago Tribune*

T0205183

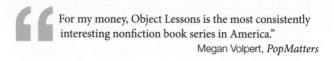

For my money, Object Lessons is the most consistently interesting nonfiction book series in America."

Megan Volpert, *PopMatters*

Besides being beautiful little hand-sized objects themselves, showcasing exceptional writing, the wonder of these books is that they exist at all . . . Uniformly excellent, engaging, thought-provoking, and informative."

Jennifer Bort Yacovissi, *Washington Independent Review of Books*

. . . edifying and entertaining . . . perfect for slipping in a pocket and pulling out when life is on hold."

Sarah Murdoch, *Toronto Star*

[W]itty, thought-provoking, and poetic . . . These little books are a page-flipper's dream."

John Timpane, *The Philadelphia Inquirer*

Though short, at roughly 25,000 words apiece, these books are anything but slight."

Marina Benjamin, *New Statesman*

The joy of the series, of reading *Remote Control*, *Golf Ball*, *Driver's License*, *Drone*, *Silence*, *Glass*, *Refrigerator*, *Hotel*, and *Waste* . . . in quick succession, lies in encountering the various turns through which each of their authors has been put by his or her object. . . . The object predominates, sits squarely center stage, directs the action. The object decides the genre, the chronology, and the limits of the study. Accordingly, the author has to take her cue from the *thing* she chose or that chose her. The result is a wonderfully uneven series of books, each one a *thing* unto itself."

Julian Yates, *Los Angeles Review of Books*

The Object Lessons series has a beautifully simple premise. Each book or essay centers on a specific object. This can be mundane or unexpected, humorous or politically timely. Whatever the subject, these descriptions reveal the rich worlds hidden under the surface of things."

Christine Ro, *Book Riot*

. . . a sensibility somewhere between Roland Barthes and Wes Anderson."

Simon Reynolds, author of *Retromania: Pop Culture's Addiction to Its Own Past*

OBJECT LESSONS

A book series about the hidden lives of ordinary things.

Series Editors:

Ian Bogost and Christopher Schaberg

In association with

BOOKS IN THE SERIES

scream

MICHAEL J. SEIDLINGER

BLOOMSBURY ACADEMIC
NEW YORK • LONDON • OXFORD • NEW DELHI • SYDNEY

BLOOMSBURY ACADEMIC
Bloomsbury Publishing Inc
1385 Broadway, New York, NY 10018, USA
50 Bedford Square, London, WC1B 3DP, UK
29 Earlsfort Terrace, Dublin 2, Ireland

BLOOMSBURY, BLOOMSBURY ACADEMIC and the Diana logo are trademarks
of Bloomsbury Publishing Plc

First published in the United States of America 2023

Copyright © Michael J. Seidlinger, 2023

Cover design: Alice Marwick

Bloomsbury Publishing Inc does not have any control over, or responsibility for, any third-
party websites referred to or in this book. All internet addresses given in this book were
correct at the time of going to press. The author and publisher regret any inconvenience
caused if addresses have changed or sites have ceased to exist, but can accept no
responsibility for any such changes.

Library of Congress Cataloging-in-Publication Data

Names: Seidlinger, Michael J., author.
Title: Scream / Michael J. Seidlinger.
Description: New York : Bloomsbury Academic, 2023. | Series: Object lessons | Includes
bibliographical references and index. | Summary: "An examination of the scream, a universal
expression that bridges both language and geography, containing the power to bring people
together and push them apart"– Provided by publisher.
Identifiers: LCCN 2022018434 (print) | LCCN 2022018435 (ebook) | ISBN
9781501386749 (paperback) | ISBN 9781501386756 (epub) | ISBN
9781501386763 (pdf) | ISBN 9781501386770 (ebook)
Subjects: LCSH: Fear. | Emotions.
Classification: LCC BF575.F2 S36 2023 (print) | LCC BF575.F2 (ebook) |
DDC 152.4--dc23/eng/20220725
LC record available at https://lccn.loc.gov/2022018434
LC ebook record available at https://lccn.loc.gov/2022018435

ISBN: PB: 978-1-5013-8674-9
ePDF: 978-1-5013-8676-3
eBook: 978-1-5013-8675-6

Series: Object Lessons

Typeset by Deanta Global Publishing Services, Chennai, India
Printed and bound in the United States of America

To find out more about our authors and books visit www.bloomsbury.com and
sign up for our newsletters.

CONTENTS

PROLOGUE

THE VOICE

A scream is the first thing we do as newborns, taking our first breaths and letting our voice punctuate the room. The loud vocalization occurs as air passes through one's vocal cords, not unlike what happens when we speak. The difference is in the force of each breath, and with that force, the scream requires that we feel with equal emphasis. When we are carried by an emotion, we push out air with such power, a balancing act between diaphragm, lungs, and throat; we rely on the resulting scream to carry a statement. For in each vocalization is a core emotion that is often distorted by the complexity of the scream's register. No matter the emotional core, it garners attention from nearby ears, urging people to take notice.

But what happens when you don't so much as make a sound?

She ran her hand through her short, curly black hair, my mother sitting with me in the waiting room of the pediatrician.

"Do you want your drink?" She holds up a Capri Sun. I look at it, but then return my attention to the Legos in my hands. I am young, but old enough to speak. Yet that's the problem. I'm voiceless, my communication skills limited to pointing with my hand, shaking my head, and when upset, bellowing out like bloody murder. It's gone on long enough that my mom has become worried, seeking the pediatrician's advice. She speaks in quick bursts. "I just don't know . . . could it be because he was a preemie?" They talk like I'm not in the room, discussing how my mom thinks I might be underdeveloped and could have an underlying mental condition. "He is easily distracted and is very hyper." It's not the first time someone's called me unusual, and it would continue to be a cause for concern. "Why won't he speak?" The pediatrician spins her chair around and leans forward, asking me gently, "What are you building there?" It's some sort of house. I offer it to her. "What is this? A house?" As is the case for much of my first couple years, people spoke for me.

I was late to my first words, even later to being able to speak with any real confidence. From birth I was silent and shy, so deeply lost in my own mind, always playing with Legos and other toys, always building things. Since I didn't have any way to explain or communicate to my parents or the people around me, I defaulted to different noises, frequent screams and shouts.

The scream is a phenomenon that many never stop to consider fully. Humans are inherently social, desiring a connection with others to relate. We have evolved into using language and the capability of voicing our thoughts, concerns, and needs. Troponyms are words made to describe the texture of a scream, using words like bawl, bellow, clamor, exclaim, roar, and more. Those words exist to attempt to capture the emotional complexity that a scream carries—and yet in each scream, there is still an uncanny openness. There's a realization: A scream doesn't require the language we have so cleverly used to communicate. All it needs is an emotional core. A deeply emotional and scared kid, I had nothing but an emotional core. The voice was something that evaded me.

I'm at the kitchen table, my plate more than half full. The rice is speckled with brown sauce, a Filipino staple, chicken adobo, growing cold as I poke at it with my fork and spoon. "Eyes bigger than your stomach," my mom says. My sister sits next to me, her plate empty. She goes for seconds and finishes that, too, while my plate stays the same. "I think he's full," she says. "Stop speaking for him," my mom scolds her. My sister drinks her milk, watching me as I begin to tear up. My mom shakes her head, "You're not leaving the table until you clean your plate." I'm pouting my lips, quickly losing my hold on my emotions. I take one bite but it's just too difficult to swallow. I choke and spit the soggy rice and meat back onto my plate. My mom rises from her seat and shouts. "Every bite! You aren't leaving the table until you eat every single bite." My sister doesn't want to leave, "But he's full!" My mom excuses her from the table and they both leave me there, crying and screaming out, the fork and spoon held between balled fists.

The pitch so bold, fear cuts like a blade—a cry is understood within seconds to be one of trepidation, a signal for potential help. Fear can fluctuate, yet its emotional core is emblematic of the scream as a cultural symbol. The scream carries out that fear, and in my case, a young boy forced to eat every bite, I just didn't want to be left alone at the table.

Eventually, mom has enough. She tests something out, effectively ruling out that I am mute, deficient in any physical sense. My mom puts a stop to everyone speaking for me, my sister and my father having learned to interpret my gestures, my frequent tantrums studded with all kinds of chortles and emotionally tinged screams. My mom says no. "They are not here to help you." She's tough, always the stern parent, but deep down she's afraid too. Her son won't speak, and doctors claim there isn't anything wrong with him. "If you want something, you're going to have to speak!" I'm left to my room, the importance of one's own voice never more important than now. My hollers and throat shredding screams do nothing. My mom shuts the door and I'm effectively grounded. It isn't until I can no longer take being left in that room that I dare to open the door, walk right into the kitchen where my mom is sitting and chatting with her sister, one of my aunts, that I make up for lost time. "Mommy, I'm hungry." A full sentence, my voice reaches them and they all look surprised. When people no longer lent their voice, I was forced to use my own.

When I finally started talking, I couldn't stop. I would go on and on about pretty much anything. Even then, though I hadn't encountered the loves of reading much less writing, I understood that there was so much to tell, and I often couldn't slow my speech enough to get it out, I stuttered and spoke with a dizzying trainwreck of anecdotes and dead ends. There was always a question.

Why is it common for most to think of the scream as something merely done out of fear or anger? Did you know that humans aren't the only species to be able to use screams as emotive devices? Hyenas use differently pitched screams as signals while hunting their prey. Foxes use a layered series of screams to communicate with each other in the night. A computer translates a scream into warning beeps, varied mechanical intonations, and capitalized letters.

My voice became something tangible and useful, though deep down, it was during those quiet years when I held back that I built an understanding and a life-long fascination for just how powerful and versatile the scream is. Be it through fear, anger, or even joy, a scream is commanding. Among these striking emotions are dozens of varieties that depend entirely on the complexity of that feeling as it brims to the surface. My early experiences with its versatility and emotive resonance influenced a deep-rooted affinity for something so abrasive yet also so alluring. It can be one of the most memorable moments in a horror film, the final girl screaming bloody murder as she drives a blade into the neck of the monster; or it could be someone on stage, the microphone held close to their lips, as they belt out a keenly practiced and complex scream that gets the crowd moshing; it could even be screams of joy as a rollercoaster rolls around the bend for its first big drop. The scream accentuates the moment. These are candid moments where the living find reason to vocalize a feeling at its most prized, the pitch of the scream hanging in the air resolute. The essence of a scream is a declaration.

My mom shouts my name from downstairs. I'm older, a 14-year-old all awkward with a face full of acne. My bedroom walls are draped with posters—an array of metal bands and Fangoria pages torn out and done up into custom vigils of some of my favorite movies. I went towards fear and anger, and it wasn't even a conscious choice. Those bands were heavy, and they screamed. I couldn't get enough. The heavier the better. Those films used to scare me, but now they had become transgressions worth the risk to prove to myself and to others that I can take it. I don't hear my mom shouting from downstairs, not at first. It takes multiple attempts. This is how we often communicated; instead of going in search of a family member, we shouted their name from wherever we were in the house. I turn down the music, catching the tail end of my mom's latest scream. There it was. I belt out my best, "WHAT?!" She screams that it's time for dinner. In that moment I get a flash of my dinners past where it ended with me red-faced, upset, throat raw from so much screaming. I now have the language to sit at that table and say, "That's enough." My plate never overflowing; I always left room for discovery.

This book will examine the depths of the scream. I want to know what else fits into a scream. Why do we find screaming so abrasive? Maybe it's far more than that, with distances as far-reaching as our own memories. From underground culture to the peak of a scientific breakthrough, and some of the most dazzling ways it informs who we are as living beings on this earth: This book will examine just how far a scream can travel to heighten a person's voice.

1 A SCREAM IN THE NIGHT

Horror made me feel alive long before I built up the courage to face my fears. Surrounded by new discoveries, being a kid with an overactive imagination often stemmed from "seeing" what wasn't actually there, be it a looming shadow figure in the corners of a bedroom or the ever-present feeling of being watched. I used to conjure mortifying nightmares about people living in the walls of my childhood home. All of this was a product of my imagination, but it came from a *very* authentic place. And that was before I had my first encounters with the manifold creations that make up modern horror.

A door closed is a tell-tale signature of a sanctuary, a quiet bedroom draped in video game posters, shelves full of action figures, a carpeted floor cluttered with game cases and controllers. Front and center, a huddled mass underneath a thick pale blue comforter. A young preteen cowers underneath the perceived armor of a blanket. The door opens. "Time for bed!" A parent giving their routine nightly command, followed by a vote of compassion. "Good night, my dear." The moment they arrive it seems like they are gone, the shadows returning. Minutes feel like hours. The preteen sweating underneath the sheets, reluctant to pull back the covers. Not even a single quick flicker of their face popping out for a peek. 9:31 PM in suburban Florida. There shouldn't be any terror dragged up from a lethargic, utterly tranquil neighborhood. The preteen has had enough, coming up for a breath of cool, air-conditioned air. Before they can take a breath, they hear it. Unmistakable, the high-pitched flaying, undeniably feminine—human or animal? No matter the source itself, the message is loud and clear.

It was a scream, no doubt about it. A scream punctuating the night quadrupled the fear already registered in my mind. The scream alone said so much, and yet it transferred an incapacitating panic that left me in my bed, cowered in all those heavy blankets, sweating it out as I imagined someone being chased by an assailant with a bloody knife. The entire image conceived from a collection of popular media I had grown up on, and yet, even at an age where I shouldn't have been such a coward, I did just that—I cowered underneath a blanket of safety.

Eventually, I built up enough to at least pass as brave. We all do as we grow older and more desensitized, lulled by far more realistic terrors. In my case, the help of Andy, my childhood friend and horror aficionado, and Capcom's 1996 PlayStation game *Resident Evil* became gateways. The latter's opening glimpse of a zombie looking over its shoulder, complete with undead moan, plus the former's peer pressure resulted in a crash course into entertainment built around fear, terror, and the threat of the unknown. Their onscreen currency was dealt in blood and gore, but more than anything else, it was the anguished, ghastly screams of terror from a starring cast that became an essential component to any nightmare soundtrack.

The iconic image of a man wearing a white expressionless mask, standing menacingly in the yard while school teen Laurie Strode catches a glimpse. Jamie Lee Curtis's onscreen debut. A glimpse of things to come. What goes bump in the night isn't any supernatural monster, it's a man with only one thing on his mind—murder. Michael Myers as trespasser takes the lives of three before Curtis is any wiser to his presence. Strode is a character written not to be easily shaken; yet seeing the bodies, she lets out a cry of horror, the first of a sequence of memorable screams. Fleeing Myers, Curtis enters a bedroom and makes a run for the balcony, only to think twice, choosing the closet at the last second. It's the setup for the legendary, brutal slasher scene. Her body balled up, knees pressed to her chest, as the heavy booted thuds of Myers gets closer and closer, the inevitable grip against the shoddy, wooden closet doors as they begin shaking, barely able to hold together as the killer continues his relentless pursuit. Curtis is on the verge of frenzy when Myers punches through the wooden beams of the closet doors. Curtis lets out painful and openly terrified cries with every punch. In a crucial act of survival, she reaches for a hanger, undoing the wire to fashion a makeshift weapon. Puncturing Myers' face causes him to drop his knife. Collapsing back into the corner of the closet, Curtis exhales relief as Myers falls to the ground.

So much of what scares us as kids still rings true when we're adults. We just get used to pushing off and dulling the fear. For so many horror fans, John Carpenter's *Halloween* is a beloved classic. The 1976 film is one of the first slashers people watch when looking to sample the genre. Among a multitude of firsts, Jamie Lee Curtis's performance is worth a direct mention, particularly with how she manages to be so vulnerable yet confident during scenes of pure trauma and menace. And those screams? Iconic.

In the decades since filming, Curtis has become revered as a scream queen, a term often given to damsels in distress in B-movie blood splatter that often do little else but fish for cheap thrills across dozens of gore-filled murder scenes. "Scream queens showcase women worrying about something other than a guy . . . unless said guy is trying to kill them," says Debbie Rochon in an interview for *GQ Magazine*. Indeed, the term has its shallow, damsel-in-distress roots, but really its heart lies in feminism. From Vera Farmiga (*The Conjuring*) to Anya Taylor-Joy (*The Witch*): The queens of today have so much to thank for those like Curtis who paved the way in those early years of screaming on the silver screen.

Curtis even recreated the shower scene in *Psycho*, originally performed by her mother, Janet Leigh, a scream queen herself, on the 60th anniversary of the film's release. Scream queens occupy an interesting cross-section of horror fandom. Perhaps it's because viewers can so effortlessly feel the onscreen terror, they forge a bond with the actors belting out those screams.

A dark room full of chills, dozens of seats lined across aisles, rows of viewers spellbound by what's playing back on the large, illuminated screen. The twin high beams of a speeding station wagon drive into the foreground, navigating the blackout of a desolate street at night. Close-up on bumpy, cratered asphalt; echoes of thunderous engine sounds. The viewers aren't expecting what the film, 2018's Hereditary, *is about to do, effectively throwing a wrench into the narrative built up by numerous theatrical trailers prior to the film's debut.*

The child star is in the backseat, struggling to breathe. Her brother was neglectful, and let the child wander the scene of a drunken teenage kegger where, without the surveillance of her brother to protect her, she ended up eating something she was allergic to. He's driving, and he's, at this point, way too drunk. The child continues her struggle, scratching at her throat as it closes. Desperate for a breath, she rolls down the car window and sticks her head out. Seconds later, the brother swerves to miss fresh roadkill, decapitating the child. The audience is still taking in the traumatic events when it cuts to the following morning, when their mother, played by Toni Collette, finds the severed remains of the child in the vehicle. The audience doesn't get to see Collette, their view

limited to the brother, the son, a mortified look on his face.
His mother's screams are so distressing it borders on obscene.
The fear in his face matches the fear shuddering across every
seat in the theater.

A scream can so seamlessly capture fear that it can be removed from its source, completely disembodied. The message remains loud. It sends chills down your spine. One must wonder why these screams are so effective. I surely did. You don't even think anything of it; the actors scream, and you feel it. Attention is often on something else, like the incoming kill, the narrow escape, or the next darkened hallway. The scream only registers later, after the feeling has already dug under your skin.

Voice actors spend their careers in the recording studio with the familiar sterile glow of studio monitors and sound proofed walls. Typically, we think of actors in sound booths reading from a script, lending their trained voices to animated characters and voice-over for commercials; however, there is a category of voice actors that earns their keep by filling in those moments of tension with a terrifying wail. Ashley Peldon is one such voice artist. A former child actress, she has lent her masterful screams of anguish and terror to everything from Bong Joon Ho's *Okja* to *The Hunger Games*. She is known in Hollywood for what she calls "rage screaming" and claims that her average day in the studio consists of a "smorgasbord of screams."

A lucrative gig? For those that do it well, sure.

"You have to totally surrender to the moment of the scene that you're in," she explains in a *New York Times* feature about the history of screaming for film. An effective scream is visceral. The best screams carry with them that emotional depth, making you shiver and hear it long after reaching the end of a film's runtime.

The key is to implant the emotional depth of a scene, so that the viewer can take the scream and fill in the blanks with their imagination. To do so, the screamer needs to be willing to be vulnerable: "You're going to feel very vulnerable at that point, and unsafe," she says. "You've let yourself go there, to your worst nightmare. I think that kind of scream, there really wasn't another way to go with it, as far as I'm concerned. You're screaming for your life."

It's actually more common for the screams on film to be added in later by people like Peldon. Jamie Lee Curtis herself has spoken in interviews about how she hasn't screamed on film for years. In fact, in the 2018 *Halloween* remake, Curtis doesn't contribute her iconic screams at all.

Treading carefully through the jungle in knee-deep water, witness a calvary of men on a missing person's search. Two men in cowboy hats carefully take their steps, the splashing of murky water creating circles in the swamp. Both men have their hands full, one aiding in carrying a woman while the other man, trailing behind, carries a rifle. His attention is focused on the water ahead. He should be more aware of hidden dangers on the riverbed, the possibility of peril itself is about to inflict upon the man's body. The viewer gets a glimpse before Wilhelm does: an interested alligator making its move. Wilhelm loses his balance due to the alligator's powerful bite, falling back first into the water. As he does, he drops the rifle and lets out a high-pitched scream.

This is the Wilhelm scream in action, featured in over 200 films. It's incredibly recognizable, and its popularity is the result of a long-running gag. The origin can be traced back to the 1953 western, *The Charge at Feather River* with a character named Private Wilhelm. Like many screams in cinema, it was recorded after principal photography, in this case performed by a looper, a person that goes in after-the-fact and rerecords sound effects that might not have made it effectively onto film the first time. The man that discovered the scream's source, Ben Burtt, found it by way of a reel labeled, "Man being eaten by alligator." He proceeded to add it to a scene in *Star Wars* where Luke Skywalker shoots a Stormtrooper off a ledge. The Stormtrooper lets out the Wilhelm scream as he freefalls to oblivion. Burtt continued to use the scream in subsequent *Star Wars* films and even the *Indiana Jones* series. The Wilhelm scream still makes it into modern-day films, including animated films like Pixar's *Toy Story*. *Game of Thrones* fans would be happy to note that the Wilhelm scream made it into the popular series. If you listen closely during combat scenes in Rockstar's *Red Dead Redemption*, some of your gunned down enemies just might let slip the Wilhelm scream. What was once a mere joke became quite the historical easter egg. There is even a band and a beer named after the hilarious audio meme.

The phone rings. "Who is this?" A young Drew Barrymore answers. The male voice on the other line flirts and skirts by her questions. "What number are you trying to reach?" Typical wrong number call. She hangs up, a slight innocent grin flashes across her face. The second call is far more curious. Again, Barrymore answers. "Seems I've got the wrong number again," the man says. She hangs up and makes some stovetop popcorn. The man calls yet again. "Oh, just some scary movie," she answers when asked what she's about to watch. "What's your favorite scary movie?" The question to end all questions, the iconic marker of the killer before he claims his next victim. Barrymore has idle hands, playing with a knife while confessing that her favorite movie is Halloween. *"You know, with the guy with the white mask." He flirts with her, eventually asking for her name. "Why do you want to know my name?" she asks. And then he says, "Because I wanna know who I'm looking at." Her nerves flare, Barrymore proceeds to be tormented by the man in the night, the security lights flicking on in the backyard. The viewers know what's coming, though Barrymore plays up the genre-standard ignorant and clueless female victim trope. Heavily sobbing, the doorbell rings, surprising Barrymore as she lets out a shaky scream.*

The *Scream* series is many things, but its best qualities are its intelligent and playful homage to slasher tropes first defined in films like *Halloween, A Nightmare on Elm Street, Friday the 13th*, and more. The name alone demonstrates the incredible value and importance of the scream as a fixture of a scary movie. In that area, there is no room for error. A scream captures our attention because it is a vessel for human feeling. So, while some screams fall flat, why do some outperform and become terrifyingly iconic?

"It must have the power to manipulate," Elena Passarello writes in her collection of essays, *Let Me Clear My Throat*. An effective scream is sudden yet layered, carrying the sort of depth that renders the human ear defenseless against the *idea* of a threat.

When I was young, I plugged my ears during the "scary parts" of a movie rather than covering my eyes. I'd rather see whatever terrifying thing than hear it.

"The best screams are like little doorways that just suck you into the movie and trap you," sound engineer Graham Reznick explains in the *New York Times* article, "They Scream! We Scream!" Horror movie screams are trojan horses of deception, the sort that once heard, you can never again unhear. It triggers the amygdala, engaging our internal fight-or-flight response.

When your mind perceives something as a threat, it triggers the amygdala in mere seconds. The amygdala, an almond-shaped structure in your brain, acts as an alarm, alerting the hypothalamus which sends signals to the adrenal glands. The sequence results in a burst of adrenaline which causes the heart to pump more blood throughout the body.

Every organ in your body reacts: lungs opening to take in more air, muscles flexing and pulsating like you're about to get into a fight. It could be loss of breath or dizziness; sweating and numbness in the hands; dilation of pupils or chest/stomach pain—the response can be overwhelming.

The woods at night. There should be three campers but one of them, Josh, went missing the night before. The morning bleeds into the afternoon, and the two remaining campers, Heather and Michael, sit around, the full weight of their impossible situation having long since registered in their minds as real, sapping any hope they may have had left. Heather sits with Michael, who rocks back and forth, before eventually speaking up with almost child-like candor: "I found some cigarettes." Heather doesn't entertain the delusion. "In the bottom of my backpack. I found some." They stick around camp all day. At night, it's all they can do to bury themselves in their sleeping bags. Then, in the distance, just a few clicks, there's an anguished scream. It sounds familiar, waking both Heather and Michael. Michael springs into action first, the fear in the screams triggering something within. Adrenaline surging through him, Michael chooses fight rather than flight. The person doing all the screaming? It's Josh! Heather knows better, readying to remain at the camp, knowing well whoever or whatever it is that's making those screams, it isn't Josh.

In both scene and sampling, Josh's screams were used by the unseen menace of the Blair Witch to beckon his friends to come near rather than back away. *The Blair Witch Project* terrified audiences nationwide in the winter of 1999 when it burst onto the scene with a brilliant mixture of organic word of mouth and a clever marketing campaign, concealing their low budget by opting for the then new and original "shaky cam" nature of the film's presentation as a real documentary. People believed it, and as they watched the black and white footage, Heather's fear-induced screams punctuating much of its hour and a half runtime, viewers like myself believed we, too, were in those Burkittsville, Maryland woods.

It helps that Heather pointed the camera on herself, often when on the verge of tears or when making some cruel discovery (like the pulled teeth wrapped in a torn patch of Josh's flannel shirt); doing so allowed those screams to be accompanied by a visual cue. The best screams can scare without revealing their source, but a scream can generate the worst fears when paired with just the right amount of human detail. Be it the twitch of an eye or the pronounced contortions the human face makes to fully express the emotion. We can thank the risorius muscle for the diverse and often unique range of expressions we can make. The muscle is located on both sides of the mouth. When someone screams, the risorius adds its own spin on the effort. Even though it might be fear, the expression doesn't necessarily always translate the same. We all make funny and odd faces when we're scared but making a face of some sort complements the fight-or-flight response produced by the delicate sequence of sensory cues onset by the amygdala. Making that face as you scream accentuates the moment of extreme feeling, thereby acting as another survival tactic.

We feel fear when we hear someone scream while being chased by a blade-wielding maniac. It makes us feel like we're the ones being hunted.

"Did you lose your shit, or do you think I lost my shit and we're just going to fuck each other up?" More than 24 hours in the forbidden zone, just past the veil called the Shimmer, their surroundings start to rewire the human brain. As the expedition falls apart, Lena, played by actress Natalie Portman, is bound to a chair alongside Tessa and Dr. Ventress. Gina has bound them for fear of something she cannot explain. She spouts missives while brandishing a knife, talking about how her fingerprints move. "If you cut me open, are my insides going to move like my fingerprints? But I'm not the one tied to a chair . . ."

Before she can do anything, a mortifying wail, almost feminine and borderline robotic, comes from nearby. Gina believes the scream belongs to Cass, a fallen teammate, and runs off hopeful of rescue. The scream is joined by a guttural bearish growl. Lena cranes her neck to the side just in time to catch a glimpse of the source of the inhuman cry: it casts an animalistic shadow against the side of the wall. A bear perhaps, but half of its face is missing, and the skin and fur is shaved off to reveal its underlying skull. The sunken eye sockets hide twin voids of a mutant mimicry. It ventures close, sniffing around, its face mere inches from Lena. Its snout twitches, letting out the recognizable scream.

Sometimes our response to that call to attention is to flee. In *Annihilation* (2018), Lena remains frozen by fear against a scream so disturbing due to how it had been disembodied, the human pulse paired with that of a dying animal.

The adrenaline response can be too much for the mind and body to handle, resulting in an amygdala hijack. The term was coined by psychologist Daniel Goleman in his book, *Emotional Intelligence: Why It Can Matter More Than IQ*, as an explanation for extreme stress when the body produces an excess of adrenaline and cortisol. In typical moments of alarm, both stress hormones would suffice for survival. In times of sitting on your couch watching a horror movie, it can result in a jolt of terror followed by an all-out panic attack. This phenomenon acts as an example of how we may have outlived practical uses for the fight-or-flight response.

In our modern-day world full of perceived and technological stressors, the fight or flight that might happen is a potent emotional reaction to something happening on social media. Still, the amygdala remains part of our minds. Screams get our attention, and horror movies are often made to be attention-getting.

There are so many recognizable encounters and tropes in these films that we unconsciously find them calmer and more cathartic alternatives to really living through fear. In some ways, they can be a sort of therapy. The emotional thrill of being along for the ride is certainly part of it—we've all been afraid of the dark, but a dark hallway in a movie hits differently than having to walk it all on your own.

Way past the point of night inching closer to late night, way past the point of any new discoveries, I am 17 and letting midnight bleed into 2AM while I listen to music, scouring different sites like Purevolume and MySpace Music. Countless bands are mere mouse clicks away from giving me another song to avoid thinking about the social pressures of tomorrow. Between songs, I sit in the silence of night, the white noise of my desktop tower fan blanketing my room with a metallic hum. Outside, crickets and heat. Summer, the heat of Florida now my backdrop, the suburban drawl of Virginia a thing of the past. My attention wavers when I get a string of new messages on AIM. I almost don't hear it. But it's there, reaching my ears, eventually registering as just what it is, a scream in the night. No blankets in sight, not this time. I leave my desk chair, glancing out the window, seeing nothing but dark houses and parked cars. It might have come from across the street. Intrigued more than anything else, I wait and listen. Then, stepping out of my brightly lit bedroom, I am on my own, the hallway dark and full of shadows. The light switch within arm's reach, I forgo the choice and navigate the house, passing by the kitchen to sneak some whiskey from my father's stash.

Only now, long after I let all those screams grace my eardrums, do I have more of an understanding of why I hated them so much as a child so painfully bound by an overactive imagination. I can play *Resident Evil* in my sleep. I dream in horror movies, walking through them like an armchair director, offering feedback on how to strengthen the impact of each scare. This didn't come easy. My friend Andy had to shove hundreds of movies down my throat, and still, I needed to find survival horror video games on my own. Becoming the characters in those games as they ran around in an all-encompassing fight-or-flight, adrenaline surging through hours of zombie attacks and demon kills—it was practice. It was a reminder that a scream calls to us, signaling that someone, somewhere, is afraid of the end, just like us. A scream is a reminder of the unknown, not too distant from the greatest unknown of all: death itself. After the act of heightening our voices to their highest octave, there can be nothing left but the inevitable fall.

We're all afraid of the end. No matter if we are willing to accept our fate—through those anguished lingering breaths, we can glimpse it in the depths of a scream.

2 STAND AND DELIVER

I wore a mask and it wasn't my own. The long dreads hung over my face, the leather gripping my skull tight enough to suffocate me. Its pale greenish-brown texture looked like something dug up from a grave. It made me look like a ghost. I *wanted* to look like a ghost.

I was 14, a shy and withdrawn goth kid that spent an extensive amount of energy avoiding confrontation. It took me months to save up for it, a near-replica of Corey Taylor's mask, the charismatic front man of the nine-member Des Moines, Iowa-based heavy metal band, Slipknot. When it finally arrived on another Friday afternoon, I grabbed it before anyone could see it and ran up to my bedroom.

The sanctuary of a locked bedroom door is no better valued than by a young adolescent afraid of the outside world. Parents busy downstairs, a teenager readies themself for the perfect fantasy: to be something they are not. They walk over to their stereo, plugging in their noise-cancelling headphones, and hit play on

*the CD currently in rotation: Slipknot's 2001 self-titled debut.
Turning up the volume, the teenager climbs up onto their bed.
The double bass clatters, the distorted guitar lays down a heavy
rhythm and groove. The teenager anticipates the first chorus.
The song is built to give listeners the perfect aggressive release.
Like the suffocating effect of the mask, the pain makes it easier
for the teenager to escape into the fantasy. To feel distant, like
an apparition. Extending an arm outward, their hand contorts
into a recognizable gesture. The metal horns held up high, the
teenager does something they typically found mortifying; they
speak up. "Are you motherfuckers ready?!" The scream is thin,
like razor blades in their throat. "Then let's do this shit!" In this
fantasy, the teenager is the leader of a band, ready to stand
and deliver, screaming pure anger to the rapturous delight of
an invisible crowd.*

From a young age, I pushed back against societal norms,
finding solace in the role of the outsider, the rebellious
spirit that preferred the less prominent path, the desire to
be left alone. I was angry, and I didn't know why. This led
me to heavy metal and hardcore. But it wasn't necessarily
the distorted guitar and frenetic music itself that enticed
me; instead, it was the voices that stood out, producing pure
adrenaline and aggression. The vocalists bared all in their
vocal performance. Often, I couldn't even understand what
they were saying, the lyrics lost underneath the roughness
of the delivery. And yet, I was attracted, quickly becoming a
life-long metalhead. To my parents, my sister, and most of my

classmates and cousins, the music was cringe-worthy. The screams were thought to be unnecessary, anxiety-inducing, and outright horrible. But to me, it was euphoric.

Performing the final song of their headlining set at Download 2009, the nine members of Slipknot command the main stage in Donington Park, England. Corey Taylor stands tall on the riser, front and center, and raises his arm. "Would you like one more song?" Unanimous cheer from the sold-out crowd. "Then are you ready to go down in history with us, one more fucking time?!" Taylor manages to draw an even louder response. "Then it's time for all of us to . . . Spit It Out!" The band launches into a fan favorite. Taylor effortlessly screams through the verse. Halfway through the song, Taylor signals for the band to stop. He shouts at the stage tech, "Turn all the fucking lights up! Let me see all of them out there!" Taylor addresses the crowd, "We're going to break records tonight . . . I need all my fucking people to get down on the ground, right fucking now." The crowd sits down. "When I say jump the fuck up, what are you going to do?" The crowd shouts, "Jump the fuck up!" Taylor waves a finger, "But not yet. Not until I say. Is that clear, you crazy motherfuckers?!" The band continues playing, Taylor timely shouting the words at the apex of the last chorus. The crowd becomes one single wave crashing and colliding into each other, the work of Taylor standing and delivering pure aggression.

My adoration came from envy and jealousy; *they* stood up on stage, didn't run away from the attention, and moreover, they willfully stood out. It was that anger, time and time again, which could be heard throughout various subcategories of the metal genre.

Maybe it was due to the stifling feeling that came from the knowledge that I couldn't face what others so easily did; the anger was more likely from the inability to feel like myself around others, less a person and more a shapeshifting shell of anxiety.

Friday afternoon in English class. The students prepare for their oral presentations, one of many assignments in the Shakespeare module; the teenager is so anxious he had thought of nothing else in the week and a half since his teacher assigned the presentation. Today is the day, the moment when students, one by one, are called to the front of the room. The teenager is a painful nervous wreck, mouth dry and voice weak, his classmates and the rest of the room a blur. It takes just 11 seconds before he finishes and flees to his desk. 11 seconds of a presentation, barely enough time to face the room. His teacher shakes her head, pure disappointment; two classmates nearby whisper to each other and chuckle. One makes eye contact with the teenager and mouths the words, You suck.

I failed both the presentation and the chance to stand and deliver. At that moment, I wanted to scream. Not out of fear, but anger. Being judged by the same people that intimidated and scared me into a corner, how was that fair? So, what if I was different? If everybody were the same, the world would be silent, missing everything but the low drawl of the same old, same old.

Second to fear, anger is deeply embedded into our psychological association with the scream. When we hear a scream, our subconscious runs to anger or fear, two sides of the same coin. And much like fear, anger causes similar physical effects—increased heart rate, elevated blood pressure, the release of adrenaline. The scream contains its own unique qualities, acoustic DNA that tells the listener all they need in a single bellow.

For generations, humans have used the scream how an animal uses yells, growls, and other variants to communicate with each other during a hunt. Once upon a time, humans did the same, long before the domestication and commodification of our waking lives, before smartphones and Uber and Grubhub. Yet the preternatural response to the scream hasn't diminished in its significance.

His name is Gunnery Sergeant Hartman, but it might as well be "archetypal angry drill sergeant." A fictional character representing a fraught act, Hartman walks up and down the line of scared recruits, one hand pressed firmly against the back of his well-ironed pristine and decorated army uniform. "Do you maggots understand?" The troops react in unison, but nothing's going to satisfy the sergeant; it's not supposed to. "Bullshit, sound off like you got a pair!" He continues to enjoy berating the recruits with an assortment of barks and orders. A recruit cracks a joke while Hartman's back is turned, the same recruit and lead character that would earn the nickname Joker. "Who said that? Who the fuck said that?!" Hartman snuffs out the culprit, every scream making his face red with anger. "I'll PT you all until you fucking die!" The threat involves an endless amount of physical training. It's a film about PTSD and the horrors of the Vietnam War; Hartman's a character facsimile of the rage that awaits the recruits on the battlefield.

Military drill sergeants utilize the sharpness of their shout, the bone-chilling swell of their scream, to evoke both fear and anger in their recruits. It is a tradition made to prepare future soldiers for the psychological and physical toll of the battlefield. Since the Vietnam War, the hostile nature of the drill sergeant may have finally faded; however, vocal methods remain intact. These harsh commands and borderline caustic drills are all part of an evolution of the battle cry.

In the heat of battle, soldiers use and articulate identifiable screams and growls across the battlefield to garner the opposition's attention and strike fear in their enemies. The battle cry is often the opening to a potential attack. The scream is as pivotal (and deadly) a weapon as any gun or blade. The battle cry drips with violence and rage, made to influence the opposition and suggest that the troop entering the battlefield has enough tenacity to be the victor.

If done right, the fear in their enemies will be enough to cloud their judgment, the perfect opportunity to gain a strategic upper hand. Long before Billy Idol co-opted the term, the Rebel Yell was used by confederate soldiers during the American Civil War to scare their opposition and boost morale. It was so effective that rumors spread. The whispers boasting that you heard the yell clearly meant you hadn't— those within earshot would not have lived to tell the tale. Imagine the anger pitched into the infamous yell, enough to manifest into a legend that endures today.

For hundreds of years, Russian soldiers shouted at the top of their lungs with a thundering "Urrah!" It was especially familiar in the trenches and battlefields of the Second World War, the opposition recognizing that Russian soldiers were near simply by the intonations of their violent scream. It was every bit a call-and-response between same-side soldiers that inadvertently scared their enemies into hiding. In both examples, we can instantly, without hesitation, hear a scream and know both what it is and the malicious anger of its intentions. But why do humans do this? The emergence of human scream analysis has lifted the veil of mystery surrounding our preternatural allure.

"Screams likely originally functioned to startle attacking predators," said Jay Schwartz of Emory University. Schwartz and his colleagues investigated how the human mind effortlessly understands the difference between "being loud" and a scream. The team had 181 volunteers listen to a random assortment of recorded samples consisting of groans, crying, moans, and, of course, screams. "We did not provide any type of definition," Schwartz boasted, who explicitly wanted to test the accuracy of a moderate sample size. In subsequent interviews, they discovered that 100% of the volunteers had the same response. In particular, the volunteers responded to the pitch—or rate of vibration of the vocal folds—of a sample. The higher the pitch, the more likely one would note it as a scream. As the vocals fluctuate from low and the rate of vibration of the folds increase, , the human ear is more likely to translate it as a scream.

"If you ask a person on the street what's special about screams, they'll say that they're loud or have a higher pitch," said David Poeppel, Ph.D. "But there's lots of stuff that's loud and lots of stuff that's high-pitched." Poeppel runs a speech and processing lab at New York University. Though pitch has its part in identifying a scream, Poeppel aspired to dig deeper. "We found that screams occupy a reserved chunk of the auditory spectrum." In their own sequence of experiments, his team uncovered the value of the "roughness" of the scream and how it played into the identification between a scream and a mere yell. The roughness is a quality that refers to the rapidity of the sound as it changes in decibels, which creates distortion. The swifter the rasp and reverberation, the more likely it will trigger the human amygdala.

"Roughness is well known, but it has never been considered important for communication," explained Luc Arnal, a neuroscientist at the University of Geneva. Arnal's team explored the extent of the roughness and potential sound triggers. Sounds were perceived as especially harsh between 40 and 80 Hz due to the range specifically requiring the engagement of new areas of the human brain to focus. "These sounds solicit the amygdala, hippocampus, and insula, in particular, all areas related to salience, aversion, and pain," said Arnal. "This explains why participants experienced them as being unbearable."

It's primal—deeply sown into our psyches. No wonder people take notice when they hear a scream. No wonder I became fascinated by 90s nu-metal.

December 1982. The chill of a wintry Manhattan barely makes it into the cramped, clustered heat of the Bowery's infamous CBGB as Washington, DC hardcore punk mavens Bad Brains take the tiny stage. Feedback from guitar amps, the low hum of Darryl Jenifer tuning his bass, the throbbing thud of the snare drum temps a crowd already inching towards critical mass. The thud gets louder, pulsing throughout the venue. "The Big Takeover" reaches its opening pop as front man HR takes the stage, grabbing the mic. Attendees swarm the stage. Within the first verse, the frenetic music matches an equally energetic crowd. HR's manic dancing inspires people to climb onto the stage and stage dive. It's intense and a sight to behold. He delivers his first lines, a shrill sing-songy bellow peppered with glimpses of distortion. "The big takeover, yeah!" Though hollow, more drapery than depth, HR's screams deliver his emotional message, as reflected in the energetic and responsive crowd.

The evolution of screaming in music is a relatively new phenomenon. Take a quick tour through music history. You will find that screams were often suggested but rarely incorporated beyond the occasional surprise. Operatic singers, for instance, staged the act of a roar but seldom taxed their own voices. It was a faux pas, and something to avoid for fear of vocal harm.

Some of the earliest utilization can be found in the work of musicians just left of center, like Screamin' Jay Hawkins, whose song 1956 hit "I Put a Spell on You," was unquestionably ahead of its time. Little Richard was a primary and early demonstrator of the vocal technique used in rock and roll. The King of Rock and Roll himself, Elvis Presley also managed to slip in some experimental bars, notably in "Jailhouse Rock." However, he seldom recreated the scream live. The same goes for The Beatles' "Twist and Shout," where John Lennon managed the swagger in the recording studio but could not replicate the vocal technique in subsequent live performances.

Leave it to heavy metal to take those early enticements and blow them out of the water. Early metal legends like Led Zeppelin and Judas Priest incorporated wails and high-pitched though clean, undistorted yells to accent their impressive voices. Robert Plant's iconic candor and Rob Halford's classically trained highs were remarkable examples of talent and skill. They exerted confidence, and they seemed larger than life, which was perfect for bands of that era. Though the scream existed in their performances, they were relegated to affectation, something to be added rather than fully incorporated into their music.

In the late 70s and early 80s, hardcore punk erupted from the depths of the underground with its raw, apathetic chord progressions, short songs (often under two minutes) with inexperienced vocalists screaming and growling into their microphones like every show was their last. It was a time when the scream was less about delivery and more about being as abrasive and obnoxious as possible—the punk aesthetic at its peak. Screaming was about denying the norm, pushing against the mainstream.

It wasn't until the 1990s and the popularity of grunge that the mainstream listener received a taste. You can glimpse pitch and roughness in perfect (dis)harmony in the textures of the forlorn grunge vocalist. Kurt Cobain drove the chorus of Nirvana's overnight sensation "Smells Like Teen Spirit" primarily using pitched screams; Chris Cornell rocketed his four-octave baritone with uncanny cries and flaunts to spice up each note. The listener might not have realized it at the time, but they were being introduced to the resonant power of the scream.

By the end of the decade, grunge was on its way out. The music industry was in hot pursuit to maintain profitable sales and general popularity in both alternative and hard rock. The machine needed more angst to feed the masses; they wouldn't need to look very far to find it. Using syncopated guitar riffs and groove-driven basslines, nu-metal extended the stylization of screaming through their aggro-driven performances. Among the first to emerge and gain a fanbase were bands like KoRn, Deftones, and Coal Chamber, which heavily utilized screaming alongside other auditory flourishes.

The audience ate it up, quick to accept and embrace more aggressive vocal styles. At the turn of the millennium, the second wave of nu-metal captivated the masses. Linkin Park, Slipknot, and Papa Roach climbed to the top of Billboard charts with hit songs like "In the End," "My Plague," and "Last Resort." At the same time, screamo—a combination of emo (highly emotional and shrill vocals) and post-hardcore, with its higher-pitched and more deliberately raspy screams—surged in popularity, due in part to alternative clothing and lifestyle chains like Hot Topic selling CDs and band merchandise and illegal music download software like Napster and Kazaa assisting in organic peer to peer discovery. With both subgenres capturing their own share of the spotlight, and satiating the youthful masses with their moody, angsty tastes, screaming became fashionable and chic.

On a warm night in Nürburg, Germany, Linkin Park closes out Rock Am Ring 2007. Mike Shinoda claps his hands, signaling the crowd to do the same. Building up to their song "Given Up," Chester Bennington approaches the edge of the stage. Faces in the crowd with yes wide; glimpses of euphoria in the thousands of fans getting to see their favorite band at their best. "I've given up. I'm sick of feeling / is there nothing you can say?" Bennington weaves through verse and chorus with practiced ease. A modest mosh pit forms to the back left of the crowd; countless bodies push against the barricade in a subconscious desire to get closer to Chester and the rest of the band. Unfortunately, they don't yet know what's about to happen. Finishing the second chorus, the band displays some of their metal influence. Bennington, draped in sweat, veins bulging in his neck, screams the words, "Put me out of my misery!" Repeating the line three times, instead of letting go of the final pitched "misery," he holds the scream, the thick rasp swelling and ongoing for 17 seconds.

Linkin Park exploded onto the Billboard charts during the peak of the nu-metal boom and quickly rose from festival opener to headlining act in under six months. Their platinum seller debut, *Hybrid Theory*, is considered a cross-genre marvel, blending hip hop, metal, and electronic music into one, well, hybrid theory of musical composition. Chester Bennington used a complex range of clean and screamed vocals. In practically every track on the album, Bennington speckled growls, screams, and other aggressive vocals to effectively convey his pain. A prominent example can be heard in the breakdown of their first single, "One Step Closer." Bennington uses a mid-range scream to shout, "Shut up!" in repetition over a distorted guitar, DJ Mr. Hahn affording the scratch and swipe at the height of every scream. Bennington's vocals were eye-opening to listeners at the turn of the millennium.

"We are the-fucking-Used!" Bert McCracken screams at a half-asleep audience, shifting between his right and left foot. His charisma and awkward yet high-energy presence are

already hypnotizing the audience. It's ten in the morning in Lombard, IL, and The Used is the first band to play Ozzfest 2003. Someone holds up a sign that reads, "SO YOU LIKE BIG TITS," but McCracken's too busy jumping in place to notice. "As we trudge along through the mud!" McCracken screams the opening line of "Maybe Memories." The audience pushes forward, pockets of space in the crowd filling in as people react to McCracken's siren call with interest, moving closer to the still relatively empty crowd. The band's quick, 18-minute set runs fast, the band playing ever so slightly more up-tempo than usual. The Used is young, new to the summer festival grind; McCracken's voice is fresh, not yet worn down from years of touring.

From the world of Warped Tour and MySpace, The Used released their self-titled major label debut in 2002 and quickly became a popular antidote for teenagers seeking a new source of aggressive release. Suddenly, it wasn't just metalheads and music aficionados enjoying screaming in their music. Like Linkin Park, The Used entered the mainstream stratosphere with renewed form and gained fans across a wide demographic.

One of the band's most important features was McCracken's vocals. Shifting seamlessly between emo-influenced clean singing and high-pitched screams, McCracken arguably achieved that tenuous balance between abrasive and accessible better than most vocalists of the era. The roughness of his screams did not fight against the listener's interest by being too overwhelming, instead doing what a well-sung chorus might do except with anger-dripping, pain-induced screams.

By the mid-2000s, metalcore and a new version of hardcore began treating vocals more like an instrument. Vocalists used a flurry of vocal techniques to produce a palatable dissonance that was less about understanding the lyrics—though the lyrics were no less essential.

Salem, Massachusetts-based metalcore pioneers Converge wrote music that might be better described as controlled chaos, with front man Jacob Bannon using mid-range growls and screams to punctuate the aural madness. Another metalcore pioneer, Poison the Well, chose to retain some melody by marrying a balance of screams and clean singing. Bands like Killswitch Engage and Underoath began doing something similar, further promoting what would become known as the "good cop/bad cop" recipe of vocal instrumentation in metalcore where screams were used for verses and clean singing saved for choruses.

Screaming added a whole new emotion to music. With it, musicians learned how to properly scream with both intensity and innovation.

On February 18th, 2014, members of the metalcore community gathered for The End is the Beginning memorial show to honor the unexpected passing of Mitch Lucker, vocalist of Suicide Silence. A dozen vocalists from different bands took turns performing tracks with the band. Small in height and stature,

Phil Bozeman walks calmly onto the stage and takes a sip of water. He glances nonchalantly at the crowd, demonstrating his comfort in being on stage. The cheers swell at the mere sight of the man, people keenly aware of his work in the band Whitechapel. A single smack of the snare, and the familiar chugging of "Unanswered" commences; Bozeman contorts into a full-body hunch, mic held at an angle as he hits the same false chord high screams as Lucker with ease. The multiple breakdowns in the song allow Bozeman to showcase his commanding lows—voluminous guttural growls that shake the floor and rattle eardrums. Bozeman stands on a riser and growls. The depth of the vocalization is so rich it receives shock and awe, and clear admiration from the audience. A master of his instrument, Bozeman demonstrates the perfect utilization of the false chord scream technique.

This library of screaming techniques has become common practice, part of the canon for anyone taking music and their instrument seriously. One of the more popular and advanced techniques, fry screams, is entirely voiceless, the sound created coming purely from the compression and closing of the vocal folds. *No* voice is used. The chords are not undulating; instead, the tissues of the soft palate in one's head and the sinuses create the distortion. This technique requires a tremendous amount of air compression from the diaphragm. The air is pushed out and passes the pressed vocal folds; when it enters the soft palate, a scream is produced. Anders Friden of Swedish Gothenburg metal band In Flames and Dani Filth of controversial death metal band Cradle of Filth are two masters of the fry scream technique.

Another technique that doesn't require the voice is called a false chord. The noise is created entirely independent of the vocal cords. The difference is in the position of the vocal folds. False chord screams and growls involve a completely open windpipe, the vocal folds never touching. When using the false chord technique, the vocalist lets air pass with most of the roughness and distortion created in the soft palate and sinuses. Corey Taylor of Slipknot uses false chord screams prominently, as does Phil Bozeman, who remains a primary example of how the false chord technique can create masterful growls, or "lows." Drill sergeants also tend to use false chord screams when galvanizing their troops.

"Heat and fire"—also referred to as a raspy singing by some vocal coaches—is a technique that deviates from voicelessness and requires extensive training to perform without vocal damage. Unlike false chord or fry screams, heat and fire uses the vocal cords and one's voice. It might be something that the listener would describe as a raspy voice or a hoarse shout. The screams are pitched while still most of the roughness is produced, once again, by the soft palate. Chester Bennington used heat and fire to create his unique pitched screams in songs like "Crawling" and "One Step Closer."

Growling can be performed using any of the techniques, but they require a distinct change in the rate and rapidity of the air being pushed out from the diaphragm. Growls rest below the mouth yet above the vocal folds. The air gestates in one's upper chest, creating the recognizable hollowness and depth of a growl. Changing the pitch of the scream is done by altering the shape of one's mouth. The assumption that "loudness" must match the roughness of a scream's quality is a common mistake that many vocalists make which often leads to early vocal strain. These techniques directly result from mastering the balance of pitch and roughness, with the volume being left to amplification from the microphone. Save being "loud" for a crowded bar at 1AM or for kids playing capture the flag in the backyard; it has no place in a musical performance. If the vocalist uses a technique correctly, they aren't in danger of damaging their voices, and the finesse will be recognizable in the depth of their vocals.

You know people are taking it seriously when an entire industry blossoms around the education and maintenance of screaming techniques. Among the first was Melissa Cross, who helped hundreds of prominent vocalists and spread the word on the legitimacy of vocals as an instrument. Now a legion of vocal coaches like Mary Zimmer and Mark Garrett teach a vast clientele of new vocalists looking to improve and understand their instruments.

The evolution of screaming occurred in just under a decade. It's crazy to see such a massive acceptance of an inherently aggressive and abrasive act. But just like in our personal lives, so much can happen in a short period.

In two years, everything around me had changed. I moved from Virginia to Florida, forced to start over at an entirely new high school during Junior year, when people had already developed their cliques and friend groups. There I was, late to the party, but I was okay with being the newcomer. I was still into metal, still listening to Slipknot. In fact, I had become even more interested in music. Nu metal had lost real estate in my bedroom stereo in favor of metalcore bands like Eighteen Visions and Walls of Jericho; punk bands like Bad Brains and The Misfits; technical metal like Between the Buried and Me and Opeth. In an act of defiance, I began to express myself by wearing attire that straddled the line between goth and gutter punk. I picked up the bass guitar and learned a few songs, but it didn't feel like the right instrument. Through friends I had made purely online, I found a professional vocal coach who trained me from afar, never in person due to my intense anxiety. She quickly saw that fry screaming would be a technique most appropriate for my stature and size. We would chat via phone and email, AIM, and the occasional snail-mail letter.

This was all before the move and the chance to start over.

The bedroom door open, the voices are magnified: the teenager isn't alone. Three familiar faces sit cross-legged on the floor, investigating the teenager's stack of CDs. They are new concert buddies, friends forged from the camaraderie of attending shows and braving the mosh pit together as a tribe. They fell into step, texting and collaborating on the next night out. But not tonight. It is a Saturday night, a slow night, a night to debate about music and listen to records. Eventually, the conversation pivots to "gateway" bands. "Probably Slipknot," the teenager says without a hint of hesitation. One friend laughs, "Really? So you started out with normie metal, huh?" Another friend sides with the statement, "Yeah, how very uncool of you." Unfazed, the teenager switches discs, grabbing the Corey Taylor mask from under the bed. "Listen and keep an open mind." The teenager switches tracks, chooses to play 'Me Inside,' and turns up the volume. The friends quiet down, visibly alarmed by the mask. The teenager climbs onto their bed, using a television remote as a microphone. "Are you motherfuckers ready?" The roughness of the scream paired with the delivery produces a response, "Yeah!" The teenager anticipates Corey Taylor's first lines, "Then let's do this shit!" In this fantasy, the teenager is the lead singer in a band, ready to scream along to Taylor's vocals. The crowd cheers, and the teenager stands tall and confidently. They deliver a performance that influences the next topic of conversation. "Dude, how do you scream like that?"

A younger version of myself would never dare scream in front of friends, much less wear an imitation Slipknot mask. But something about others being there no longer mattered. I was going to rock out with or without their approval. I managed to keep up with Taylor, the look of shock and astonishment on their faces was validation of my angst, a release not unlike euphoria, adrenaline surging through my body. As I stood and delivered my performance, I felt whole.

I didn't turn away from fear. My response was my battle cry. *I'm right here motherfuckers. This is who I am, like it or not.*

I was wearing a mask that I didn't originally design, screaming along to a song that I did not write. But the angst was my angst and the screams were *my* screams.

Letting go meant finding myself.

3 STEP FORWARD, SPEAK UP

I was 14 when I lost my best friend. Don't get me wrong—he's still alive. His life continued after the dissolution of our friendship. In a way, my life didn't, or at least it felt like the end. Losing a long-time friend, your first real best friend, especially when you're highly introverted and meeting new people is so very difficult, it feels so much like the worst of all possible scenarios.

I was always so hard on myself, seldom cutting myself any slack—that "glass half empty," never to be filled, highly critical view on life. My parents were hard on me. My mom always told me I had to prove to myself and the world that I was worth the breath of a bright new day or else I was a waste of space, a failure. It worked. It still works. I overextend and exhaust myself, my work/life balance usually in constant flux. And I would gladly lose touch with people if it meant more hours spent working on this book or the next.

After we got caught for something that had been my idea from the start, I became the mastermind who backed off during the moment of truth. I should have been ready to argue and stand up for the cause. Instead, I lost my voice. Had I tried to open my mouth, nothing would have come out. Worst of all, I didn't stand up for my best friend.

The list is a page long. Assignment titles, class, and letter grade. Effectively a transcript with three recurring names, all of them suspect. Three names – B. Love, O. Stamp, K. O'Connell. Three classmates on the starting football team, prized and favored among so many of the student body, untouchable. A Catholic private school carries with it a certain privilege. Speak only when spoken to. Nope, that isn't going to work for me and Christopher. Not for two rebellious outsiders, goth in any sense of the term, but in most circles circa 2001, goth as in "loner." Not today, another afternoon in early February, the frigid chill still in the air. We weren't going to stand for it. Physical Education ended, and with two periods left, we stood back. We were late to change out of our PE uniforms, intentionally, because we had a plan. We had a secret.

Some things you must stand up for. Nobody should be able to get away with stealing essays and blackmailing other members of the student body simply because they believed they were "more important." Their bullying and common scare tactics were enough to get other students buckling under the weight of their own influence..

We waited until our P.E. teacher did his routine locker room check to look for any stragglers. He finally showed up right as the five-minute bell for the next period rang. Christopher stepped forward, offering the opening line: "Mr. Hall, can we talk to you for a minute?"

We did it as a means of protest. Enough was enough. Christopher was one of the students bullied and blackmailed into essentially taking on double the course load, his and Love's. I was barely a dot, none of their concern, but behind closed doors, I made it personal and got involved, enjoying every minute of the case being built against those power-hungry footballers. When the time came to back all our efforts with justifiable action, Christopher stepped forward while I stepped back. I clammed up while Mr. Hall dissected the list. Eventually, the provost called everyone to their office to clear the air and get to the bottom of the matter.

You can imagine how that went.

Christopher stuck his neck out, and the bullying worsened as the football players became better adept at their concealed threats. He never spoke to me again. Not during the rest of that semester, not after word got around school that I was relocating to Orlando, Florida.

I wanted to scream.

We've all been there, the surge of emotion bubbling up to the surface, so intense you could break out in hives. Then, letting out that vicious bellow of disgust, full of high-punctuated feeling, the moment following the scream—pure relief. That's precisely what stepping forward and taking a stand feels like.

Millions of people that have taken to rally—whether to protest Trump, the turmoil in the Middle East, or pretty much anything in the political ecosphere—know well the release that comes from picketing and backing an issue with heated screams, especially when your roars are matched by a crowd of like-minded protestors.

A scream acts as a central tenet of political protest. It is hard to ignore and does wonders for delivering a message, even if the message itself is muted by your surroundings. The dynamic of a protest is such that the passion around us is matched by the force in our lungs, the furor of our message. Bubbling from the depths of our throats, it doesn't matter if we're screaming correctly. We're still going to scream. Those screamed chants are illustrations of hope. They exemplify our disgust, with something better hidden just below the abrasive caterwaul.

"Belief and expectation—key elements of hope—can block pain by releasing the brain's endorphins and enkephalins, mimicking the effects of morphine," explains Jerome Groopman, a doctor and staff writer at *The New Yorker*.

Even if those receiving your screams of disgust are ready to take them and form an argument of their own, there's hope trailing the end of those screams.

The act of stepping forward empowers an individual.

There's no way you're backing down now. Your voice has been heard.

It can be infectious. Politics are almost always taken personally. Civil debate walks a thin line between turns and timed responses. Sometimes things can get heated quickly.

A lacquered oak table is set with matching silverware and a pleasing light-blue tablecloth; six placemats set, awaiting the night's guests. An array of savory and sweet smells billow from the kitchen as one of the hosts answers the door. The wine is poured the moment the guests settle around the table, sampling cheese from a charcuterie board and making small talk to break the ice. A second pour brings out a more salacious conversation. Two guests talk about a mutual colleague botching their hand in the most recent project deliverable, setting the entire team behind another week. One guest takes large gulps from their glass and steers the conversation into the current political election. They are very adamant about their side and make it clear after politely standing their ground as the other guests attempt to fire up a debate about ICE, deportation, and border control. Maybe it's the wine talking, but the guest simply won't hear it, raising their voice when the co-host enters the room with a few appetizers, unaware of the sudden shift in conversation. The guest shakes their head when the co-host asks if they might change the subject. "No, no, I won't. You see, look, you can't just listen to Twitter! Twitter is an echo chamber. They aren't showing both sides. Everyone's either a liberal asshole or a republican asshole!" Another guest, quiet until this very moment, sets their glass down next to their plate and calls the argument "baseless." Guests exchange glares; they now have a standoff. The guest that started it all is noticeably red in the face. Voices are raised to match the rapidity of each guest's comments until you can't hear anything over a smear of words launched violently with vicious shouts of revulsion.

Sound familiar? We've all been stuck in those uncomfortable social moments. A shouting match exists when a debate or public discourse bursts into extreme, often defensive remarks between participants. Seldom does it seem like a match in the strictest sense because the participants tend to project their voices over each other. Such displays were standard during the 2020 United States presidential election. Rarely making any clear points, the presidential debates saw Trump and Biden devolving into a shouting match: mean-spirited comments tinged with the faintest note of a shout.

A scream is so powerful that it can be used as a weapon. Much like a battle cry, the act of screaming can influence an argument. Never to be outdone by negativity, the protest can use screams for inherent good.

During a mild spring day in May, a press conference is set up outside the Belarusian embassy in Warsaw. 28-year-old Jana Shostak walks with a sign held high above her head. SOS is painted in red and white. A sea of journalists waits for her and others to speak. The mics are primed and pointed upward as she steps forward. For one whole minute, she screams blood-curdling, throat-searing screams, her skin turning pink before turning red. Her lungs gasping for air, she takes a second to inhale and immediately lets out another lengthy scream. Veins bulge in her neck; the risorius muscle in her face causes her jaw and lips to accentuate her disgust, mouth and cheeks outstretched to exemplify how much those screams hurt. Yet they don't hurt as much as what has already happened—her fellow activist's arrest due to Nexta, a messaging application, releasing communications which organized protests against Belarusian President Alexander Lukashenko's continued silencing and repression. The charges could carry up to 15 years in prison. Many of the activists have been painted by the media, influenced by Belarusian authorities, as extremists. "We can't be silent anymore, and all we have left is a minute of screaming." Stepping forward because people are being ignored. Stepping forward because people are dying. Stepping forward because people have been viewed as less.

Shostak used her screams to voice her disgust for the Belarusian opposition movement in Poland. Labeled a terrorist by the government-influenced media, Shostak was an activist backed into a corner. "I'm scared for my life . . . in the Belarusian media I was officially labeled a terrorist [and] for days now I have been seeing undercover protection from Belarus with a characteristic VHS that they use to record everything," she told Interia, a large Polish web portal. Still, she stepped forward and spoke up: "This will not silence me." Her protest might not be fearless, but it is one fueled by complete disgust in how her country's government officials failed their people. Her screams were videotaped and uploaded online, going viral, precisely the opposite of what detractors and authorities hoped to keep silent.

"Get outta town, fucking treasonous pieces of shit." 60-year-old Peter Tracey, a lawyer living near downtown Washington

D.C. stands on the front stoop of his house, screaming at the top of his lungs at rioters fleeing the pro-Trump rally planned to transpire at the Capitol building on Wednesday, January 6th, 2021. A bystander captures his vicious outcry using their smartphone and uploads it to Instagram and Twitter. The video goes viral. In it, Tracey appears initially calm before quickly spouting profanities. His screams of disgust at the sight of Trump banners draped down the side of passing vehicles strikes a nerve, Tracey breaking the citywide request made by mayor Muriel Bowser not to engage in any matters involving the rally. "If you want to walk through my neighborhood, as the people I was screaming at did, with your Trump banner unfurled—well, in my mind, you've opened the door to my fair comment on your position."

Tracey would have followed mayor Bowser's statement and kept silent, but it was the Trump propaganda that pulled him to step onto his front stoop and express his disdain. They made it personal, or perhaps it was always personal . . . the protestors entered his neighborhood with the animosity of a politically charged strike.

In the case of both Tracey and Shostak, the scream is used as a powerful weapon in manners that are heartfelt and dire. Unlike the vitriol of a shouting match during a political debate or political dictators that might use the weapon as an attack, most people have a sense of their own voice. You seldom need to, knowing well that to register the roughness, the full pitch of a painful, angry, or perhaps disgusted bellow would mean you have an emotional response and reason to step forward and speak up. Injustice so deeply felt made Shostak and Tracey do something about it.

The potency of a human's need to believe in something—to know that there is more to the sum of their days—and placing one's own systems of order and understanding into teachings of scripture, it is a human necessity. We *need* to believe in something. The strength of one's emotional outcry carries eerily similar conditions across both a political and religious scream.

It's Sunday mass and every pew is full. A priest, middle-aged, slight grey in his short hair, stands at the podium. The readings have concluded, and in praise of the Lord Jesus Christ, the priest is tasked with speaking wisdom and faith. The sermon begins slowly and calmly, a story about someone's beliefs being tested. The priest recalls details from the mass's readings, different passages memorized, the story about how God tested Abraham's faith by telling him to take his son, Isaac, and go into the mountains and sacrifice him in the name of the Lord. And then he speaks candidly: "I have had my faith tested long before I knew that the Lord would never leave my side." The more personal the sermon, the louder his speech; some words like "testing" and "hurt" are shaky in tone. The priest has the microphone linked to the podium, but he backs away, pacing around the stage, no need to use it. His voice now an all-consuming candor, he has the entire congregation listening to his story of when he failed one of God's tests, abandoning his faith for the bottle, abandoning his prayers for the lonely dead-end power-hunger trip that was the music industry. He had been a heavy metal musician and had played shows that made him feel like a god. "Maybe I believed it!" Soon his own self-hatred, a time when he would have rather committed suicide than turned to scripture and God for guidance, causes tears to well up and run down his face. All that's left is for him to scream, letting out all that pent up scorn, all that old and cobwebbed disdain. His screams launch from the breadth of his lungs. "Turn it into something good. Turn it into prayer!" The congregation stands up and replies, "Amen."

The power to do something; what about the power of faith?

The priest, so very inspired by the force of his faith, needed more than mere language. His sermon evolved into cries of valor and praise, the screams sounding blissful on the verge of a rallying cry. But this isn't unusual, not when at the base of each breath is emotional strength at its tipping point. There could have been no other reaction.

A mournful crowd walks a green field on an overcast Sunday morning. Everyone's wearing black, walking two or three at a time, everybody headed for the same destination, everyone thinking about how unfair one's duration on this planet, and in life, can be. Though many would prefer to cry silently, sobbing in each other's arms, the controlled chaos of their collective screams is enough to startle and scare any unsuspecting creature. Their wails are pure, unadulterated prayer, carrying on for the entire walk to their common bond, the death of a family member, someone so very close and dear to them. They cry out not just because they can't stand the misery they are feeling, but also because of the awful truth of a life taken way too early, at just 20 years old. Their screams are a testament, a protest to whatever higher power might be listening. They were so young; why did you take them? When they reach the casket and future grave of the deceased, the screams don't stop. They continue until every person is an example of complete emotional and physical exhaustion.

Keening is a death lament, an Irish oral tradition from sixteenth-century Scotland. Keening over the recently deceased, especially during the funerary procession and from the burial site, is done to express the woeful condition of those who must endure the loss. Though the tradition usually involves only a handful of women close to the deceased, larger and more expansive choruses and vigils have grown to include a wider audience.

Keening has its roots in human's relationship with death and the afterlife. The severity of our emotional condition after losing someone—there is rarely a more saddening feeling. Those found at the crossroads of loss can feel dejected as much as they can feel enlightened. The elements thought to be invisible and imaginary are suddenly made visible.

In some religious practices, a similar vocal lament becomes an instructional tool for those seeking higher consciousness and being.

Draped in a ceremonial robe, a Zen master offers a tutorial to a small group of willing participants. "Trust that you are alive in this moment. Trust in your gut." He oozes confidence and openness, taking his time in explaining what he's about to do. The world outside the room seems to drift away. "You are sitting on a cushion, listening." He talks about how to refuse passing judgment and be in the moment. There's some explanation about how the "shout" is supposed to come from your abdomen, and it's supposed to generate and pull from that part of your body so that your energy "comes down." Your energy all comes from the brain, and you can't live life only in your head. You need to let it out. You need to "come down." He instructs the class to inhale, hold for three seconds, and then let it out. It sounds intense, almost like a fighter throwing a punch, a "hi-ya" of sorts. The class does this for a few minutes, and when it's over, you can feel the energy in the room release, a full swath of relief.

Katsu means, literally, to shout in Chinese. It is a scream made open the mind and body to the process of enlightenment. You might not get there if you continue to judge both yourself and your peers. Actions are made to be actions first, a wise choice to exist in that moment. Katsu is a Zen practice made to maximize what a scream can do to the body: release disgust and tension. It's meant to make you feel alive.

Four women wearing green dresses and head wraps stand in front of a receptive audience. It's deafeningly quiet in the room.

They inhale and exhale in unison, a whole minute passing before they open their mouths and let out a sing-songy scream. It continues, the screaming, in rhythm with their stomps and claps. They press their hands to their heart and then their chest, letting out nearly incoherent words hiding in the depths of their scream. They turn and gyrate, scream-singing with enthusiasm. They are doing this for their faith; they exemplify the fullness of their spirit. It's clearly infectious because the audience steps forward and speaks up too, offering their own screams to the women's performance.

In African rituals originating from slaves in the United States, ring shouts were popularized by a group stomping and clapping their hands while screaming and really putting their heart into it. It has come to modern practice simply as a shout or spout of controlled screaming in modern day Black and non-Pentecostal church assemblies.

There are similarities between the Zen katsu and the African ring shout. Both are physical exercises designed to release energy to heighten the mental faculties and become closer in spirit.

What about speaking in tongues? So often it's used in horror as an exemplification of an invading demon, the devil possessing you. However, its roots are in the same place as any of the aforementioned religious and ritualistic screams. It's merely a matter of letting all that emotion loose, breaking free of judgment and disgust, and letting your physical limits be tested. In this case, it's not about your voice; it's about what your lungs and abdomen can produce.

Screaming can be sacred.

She's alone in her bedroom. It's night, late enough that she lets out a yawn and then a second one. Slowing her breathing, she presses a finger to her neck, feeling the vein pulse. When she's ready, she knows already that this won't be something considered normal, and yet she doesn't care. She's not supposed to. It's about naturally letting go, letting herself go free with the Lord. Time to demonstrate her faith. She starts by saying a prayer completely in a whisper. When the prayer is completed, she says another prayer. The same one, repeated. Another repetition. With each utterance, she raises her voice. Soon it transfers from the throat to the diaphragm. The pit of her stomach runs deep, her abdominal muscles clenching as the prayer becomes muffled in her shouts. Soon it's a loud sequence of screams, the prayer melding into something that no human being could understand. They sound like words, but they might be a gospel from the underworld. She continues doing this until her body gives out, fresh sweat glistening on her forehead. Falling onto the bed breathlessly, she wheezes, lungs desperate for air.

The medical term is "glossolalia," but in any definition of what was just sampled, it's speaking in tongues. Should language fail the individual, they can turn to one of our most basic and reliable acts. Speaking in tongues has little to do with the horror and "possession" that Hollywood has popularized in films like *The Exorcist* and *Paranormal Activity*. The act is similar to a ring shout—physical strain giving way to pure emotion. In the end, it's always about raising your voice.

Commonly used as a warning or command, parents say it to scold their children. But we speak when we believe in something. We do it as a ritual, as an act equally defiant and based in our adamance for something, be it political or religious, personal or public. Ultimately, if you have anything to say, you have to first believe it's worth the effort of saying it outright.

Speak only when spoken to.

I guess I just wish I had, all those years ago.

Mr. Hall's voice almost always sounds like nails on a chalkboard. Lots of rumors float around about how he tried to kill himself once. He has a noticeable scar wrapped around his throat; probably why he always wears garments that hide his neck. Hanging yourself leaves a mark. Chris can't stop looking at it as he hands him the list. It's the first time we see his neck bare, plain and simple. The rumors are true. But that afternoon, urgency isn't on suicide, though Chris is about to do something. "Umm, so we have this." I'm stepping back, back against the lockers. Voiceless, Chris giving me that look, the one that says, What are you doing? Come on, say something! *But I leave him in the cold to do all the tattling. Mr. Hall opens the list, glancing at it. "Where did you get this?" Chris doesn't answer the question. Instead he says, "They've been using people. They blackmail us. I swear it's true."* Maybe he shouldn't have said that last part. Mr. Hall has, like all faculty, has some involvement in the football team, meaning their success is something to proudly display their own success; the school's success is their success. Mr. Hall folds the list. Chris watches him fold the list. I watch Chris watch him fold the list. And then he tears it up with a sigh. Mr. Hall doesn't look at me when he says to Chris, *"You're coming with me."* It's like I'm not even there.

I didn't step forward. I didn't speak up. We all still got in trouble. Detention for two weeks. They still blackmailed students into doing their work. They continued bullying people even after the football season was over and they made it to the playoffs. It was all so meaningless, yet I still think Chris maintained that he did it for the right reasons. It most definitely garnered respect in the entire student body. The way everyone looked at me after the fact, or rather, didn't, like I was invisible—it hurt just as much as losing Chris as a friend.

I wish I could have stepped forward and spoken out. I want to scream out my apology, but it's already too late. So I'll do the next best thing. I'm going to apologize, right here, in the pages of this book. Stepping forward and speaking up. My words might be **bolded** or CAPITALIZED, but, in each line, here, my screams of apology, self-disgust for cowering in fear, they exist on the page. I AM SORRY. I AM **SO** SORRY.

This could be enough. I have to believe it, deep down in my gut, that the apology might be heard by you.

4 I HAVE NO MOUTH, AND I MUST SCREAM

Everyone talks about the joy of creativity and how being an artist is about expression and a connection with an audience. The last part may be true, but for the longest time, it's what I worried about most. Being able to express myself was so exhilarating it was worth life itself. But the part about having to speak to others about my art? Mortifying.

My biggest fear was being seen.

Speaking up is one thing, but standing on stage, being interviewed or asked about your process, being in the spotlight at all, gave me enough anxiety that I suffered from constant panic attacks. During high school, I could barely hold it together facing a class of 25.. It took so many years to build a bridge out of that black hole of anxiety.

Maybe that's why I turned out to be a writer. Thing is, nobody tells you that to be a writer, you'll have to do plenty of public-facing events like readings and interviews. What happens when I'm supposed to get on someone's podcast or be asked to speak to an audience of strangers? It was enough to make none of this worth it. I loved the creativity part. There's such a dynamic pleasure to being able to commit to your craft, and not everyone gets a chance to speak about their art. Still, I dreamed of being some reclusive writer, a Thomas Pynchon type, and desired to never tweet, never talk, never even raise my voice. Instead, I signed up for Twitter and started reading into the lives of artists.

How did they manage their anxiety? What made them scream out in pain and sadness?

The more I learned about the lives of my favorite artists, the more I recognized that their art was a cry for help, a vessel for projecting their screams into the sadness and despair of every day, especially when they doubted their own work. The more I learned, the more I saw a reflection of myself. Turns out maybe art chose me.

"Some days are better than others." I am sitting in the small, cramped studio apartment of a writer I admire, A. His desk is pushed up against the largest window, giving him a view of a brick wall. The desk is piled high, four, maybe five books deep, and there are wrinkled and coffee-stained manuscript pages riddled across the entire surface. A sits in his peeling leather chair, downing the rest of his whiskey. I brought a bottle. This was supposed to be an interview. When I arrived, he cowered at the thought. "Can't we just talk?" Fine. I figured I could take down everything I managed to remember. That was before all the whiskey, long before our talk lengthened late into the night, books and craft, craft and books. He never spoke

any louder than a low hum, almost a whisper depending on the topic.

At one point, I ask him about his distance from the public, why he is so shy and withdrawn. "I wasted my voice early. I'm selfishly keeping what's left for myself." I didn't quite understand; but then again, I was really drunk. We both were, though A didn't let it on. Eventually, he started dozing, so I took my leave. But A's explanations revealed some truth: A had success early, outspoken for a time. Big book with the Big Five. Even bigger advance. Everyone talked about it. Then it didn't do as well, perhaps because he was too loud online. Too quick to respond to trolls. ALL CAPS. All screams, all the time. "Can't we just talk?" He was so afraid. Maybe there are limits to a scream, just as there can be a limit to how much sadness a single being can endure.

A continues to write and hasn't returned to public life. That night, the look on his face when I asked if it was okay to record the conversation using the app on my phone, that look of dejection coiling at the edges of his forehead: It reminded me of *The Scream*, the famous painting that everyone knows about. It influenced a myriad of artists and copies, including the Ghostface mask in Wes Craven's influential *Scream* meta-horror franchise. *The Scream*, a masterpiece of expressionistic art. Think about it for any more than a second, and it's the same thing all over again: wondering about the artist's process, the inspiration, and meaning behind such a monumental work of art.

Edvard Munch, what were you thinking? What are you trying to say?

There can only be one focal point. The lone subject's details are second to the emotional expression that iconized the entire piece. Eyes glaring off to the left, at something or perhaps everything, this individual is perhaps terrified at an invisible force, one that we reckon with every day. Hands pressed against their cheeks, the subject exhibits the emotive potential of a scream. Wearing long bluish garb, much like their facial features, long and under-developed, as though the ennui and despair have blurred out the through-line. Orange and red and yellow streaked across the sky, with the would-be pristine blue waters of the surrounding river, this subject is on a boardwalk or bridge, on an excursion that should be relaxing. And yet . . . what is this figure running away from? What do they finally see, admitting that both the fear and the sadness is worth the scream? Two people off in the distance, might they hear it, or is it a silent scream, the sort that doesn't so easily wash away?

The painting is one of our most essential displays of a prevailing human condition.

History tells us that Munch had been out on a walk at sunset when the initial idea for the painting came to him. That moment of eureka, seeing how the setting sun caused the light around him to turn a blood-red. So unexpected, he wrote in his diary that what he felt most of all was an "infinite scream passing through nature." People would later fixate on the reason for the blood-red sky. There are many theories shared among art scholars—ranging from a volcanic eruption to something more psychological—but the inspiration ultimately doesn't matter. What matters most is that Munch was inspired. He quickly set to work on two versions using pastels and lithograph stone. It wasn't for any other drive other than to take the inspiration and chase after it, expressing that moment of absolute sadness.

Munch could have merely screamed, but instead, he used paint to capture the infinite scream. It's no wonder *The Scream* became so fascinating and popular: We all feel this way, more often than not, pressures flanking us through thick and thin. Art imitates life, and life can be so very sad.

45 minutes. That's how long it lasts. The performance baffles everyone long before they become addicted to it. This is Marina Abramovic in 1975, performing a piece wherein she must damage her voice. Laying upside down, head tilted back, neck craned in such a way that her chin points straight up, perpendicular to the hard surface that becomes her bed and coffin. The blood quickly rushes to her head. Her mouth a gaping wound, she starts low, letting the despair-induced wails rise high until you can hear her throat buckle, false chords clenched shut, rubbing against each other. She looks like a ghost; the sounds that accompany this devastating performance are that of sadness itself, calling out to anyone within earshot to look inward and see where all that despair has welled up. Scream, why don't you? Scream! Perhaps it is what Marina is doing, screaming for us. Allowing physical pain to replace all that emotional toil built up over the years.

In *Freeing the Voice*, the simple and direct title of the piece, Abramovic uses her body as the canvas. Specifically, her voice becomes the metaphor, the vessel that falls apart for its viewers. Toward the end of the performance, her voice stops sounding so harsh and rough, typical of a commanding scream. She begins to have trouble pushing through the pain. The hoarseness in her voice limits her ability to produce that message, and yet she continues to scream. The screams almost take on the texture of breathless moaning. Those watching would have to fight back the urge to save her from herself. But that's not the point, is it? *Freeing the Voice* is just that: freedom. Because in feeling all that physical pain, she no longer can entertain the despair.

Art doesn't imitate life, in this case. It *is* life.

Fans of A Streetcar Named Desire gather at the end of the Tennessee Williams New Orleans Literary Festival for a "Stella Shouting Contest." A tradition of sorts, it's about seeing who can best do what Marlon Brando did so many decades ago. That irrefutable and utterly recognizable chortle, screaming out from the gut, but more than that, streaming out from the heart, Brando's complete lack of training resulted in one of popular culture's most recognized screams, parodied across time. In no time, it seems, everyone gathers around an unmarked patch of asphalt, almost like they're about to take part in a fight club.

Instead, people wearing their best Stanley homage, complete with the trademark white shirt, the surrounding area of the French Quarter is full of unwitting recipients of dozens of contestants doing their best to capture that pain of loss and loneliness that Brando captured so well. "STELLLA!" People laugh at one particularly animated contestant's rendition, who grabs at his shirt, on the verge of tearing it. "STEEEELLA!!!" The audience gasps at another, who throws himself onto the asphalt, scraping his skin, resulting in a little bloodletting. STELLA! The crowd waits for their own turn, and it's all while hearing these entries in succession that the screams blur together, almost like they aren't hearing anything at all except the moment extending to include all those that are present that day to honor Williams, but also to honor the inevitable heartbreak that comes with opening yourself up to feeling. "STELLLLLA . . ." A contestant interprets the scream more openly, somber and standing there almost lifelessly, screaming into his chest. In doing so, he seems to cry out, leaving behind any roughness to his vocal intonation. Instead, he captures what this is all about: the desire for human connection.

The people that chose to take part in the competition are more playful, maybe hobbyists in nature; but they're using their bodies as extensions of their inner sadness. It isn't wasting time; it's being part of something. It's about not being alone. Lonely perhaps, but we all are, at our core, saddened by the reality that we're alone in facing our demons, our challenges; that despair that creeps in when you least expect it. The competition closes out an entire festival whose main point is to keep Tennessee Williams's work alive. By the time the contest is over, the ringing in your ears and the sudden silence is an undeniable reminder that at some point in life, we all must face our inherent aloneness.

In the wake of the festival, there is silence, just as in the wake of experiencing a work of art; you feel so very open and vulnerable to your own emotions. Yes, things hold a different weight—suddenly everything is so very vivid and unyielding.

Leuven, Belgium, May 26th, 2009. A notable rumbling emanates from Predikherenkerk, a Dominican church. On the other side of those walls, the space is almost completely concealed by thick fog, as though the sound being created onstage is opening a portal into another dimension. On stage, three musicians wear hooded robes, standing in front of a wall of stacks. The musicians hold up their instruments to the stacks, creating a noticeable hum of feedback. Even if the crowd wanted to cheer, their voices wouldn't puncture the wall of sound the band is cultivating from the ground to the rafters of the church. Everyone's here to experience Sunn O))). It's less about listening. The band begins amplifying the sound—layers of what might be the sound of manmade instruments growling duel against the piercing roughness that sounds like a saddening scream. This goes on for over an hour, the blanket of artful, completely manmade screams delivered in a droning wave.

The Seattle, Washington-based band is no stranger to deafening concerts and controversial critical reviews of their work. The band is well known in some musical circles, while in others they occupy a similar space as other hard-to-swallow, difficult-to-understand projects like Michael Gira's Swans or even Oneohtrix Point Never's more chaotic earlier work.

It can all be threaded to a very different kind of music. Call it drone. Like any accurate tag or label for something, it captures its essential ingredients with seemingly effortless simplicity. Drone. That's totally a good indicator to describe a Sunn O))) performance. Yet, there are many different categories of drone. It's a surprisingly diverse style. Some artists aim to create soothing landscapes of sound, something that might not be far off from the sound of a baby snoozing, while others aim for aural violence. Drone is layered sound. Not quite guitars and bass and drums playing to a rhythm, yet there can sometimes be the faintest arrangement of a rhythm hidden behind a wall of sound. But that's ultimately not the point. Artists turn to drone music to capture a feeling. It can capture ecstasy as much as it can capture sadness.

The sound created can best be described as mechanical, not a human pitch; but what these soundboards and manmade mechanical instruments are doing is the same as your lungs and throat—screaming out to be heard. Screaming out to feel and hopefully capture others in the act of feeling. This style has to do less with performing fully defined and discernible "songs" and more with providing an entry point into another world. This is audio at its most imposing, with the aural cacophony of droning performances carrying the same ingredients of a sharp, eardrum-scarring scream.

When listening to the darker corner of drone, where elements of other musical genres like black metal become an influence, the wall of sound takes on properties of palpable darkness. In all that violence, the hum and the buzz, the growl that vibrates so deeply you can feel it in your own stomach when witnessing it live, you are hearing sound itself scream.

A silver fighter jet sits on the tarmac, a few crates tossed around, many of them used as improvised seats. Pilots and other Navy gather, everyone watching the rounds add up on a street fight. Not just any street fight either. This is Street Fighter II, *and there's a red 1980s boombox on the ground, a few beer bottles, and at least two voluptuous feminine spectators, just to fill out the stage for the key demographic for a fighting game in 1991. Since each character gets their own stage, this one must be Guile's. He's down a round and trying to gain ground on his opponent, the franchise icon and nomadic warrior, Ryu. Both fighters block and attack, grunt and let out confident attack bellows, but when Guile finally gets his opponent launching endless fireballs from near one of the stage's larger crates, effectively the edge of the stage, backed into a corner, Guile knows what he needs to do. Guile pairs up Sonic Booms, his own flash-fireball signature move, against Ryu's effortless fireballs. Baiting him to jump forward, the fireballs and booms are launched and landed, negating each other before they can make any real impact. Frustrated or maybe tired of doing quarter circles, Ryu takes the bait and jumps into the air, trying to get closer to Guile, who had been crouching, priming up his even more iconic flash kick. Ryu goes for a fierce jump kick, but it is cancelled out by Guile's flash kick. Life bar down to zero, Ryu lets out a distraught death scream.*

So many video games are violent, that much is true; and yet they do a wonderful job of capturing the authenticity of the moment. Even at the indie level, game production values need to be peak, one of the biggest portions of the gaming budget pie. A gamer isn't just watching the thing, after all. They are in it. Developers need to think about stuff like frames, reaction times, input delay, replay value, and game-breaking design loopholes. Amid all the design, programing, and balancing, game production carries an additional set of essentials such as an appealing UI (user interface), refined graphics, and, of course, equally refined sound design.

Much like the principles drone artists utilize to create sound from scratch to add to a layered aural experience, video game composers and sound designers use the full gamut of vocalists, soundboards, and synthesizers to create the sounds littering the cacophony of, say, a battle in *Street Fighter II*. Though the individual ingredients might come from a human being, the effects are processed through mixing and mastering, often processed into smaller file sizes so that it can all fit on a game cartridge or CD. But that's what's so amazing about game sound design, perhaps a less regarded artful example of the scream.

Playing all those matches of *Street Fighter II*, winning and losing hundreds of times, the final strike followed by the death scream of your opponent, players are not only feeling the euphoria of a victory; they are subconsciously learning to understand the complexities of competition. A seasoned *Street Fighter II* player recognizes the pangs of pain, anguish, and sadness in the knockout screams of their opponents. Like Ryu bellowing before falling to the ground with a heavy thud, bruised and broken, they have the full recovery, both emotional and physical. The Sisyphean task of yet another battle bursts with adrenaline and pain, loss and failure, to endure.

Good sound design conveys all of this in a single tiny soundbite played back ad nauseum, without ever losing its emotional impact. These sound effects are screams from the depths of silicon.

It is surprising what might come out of their shell, if given the right conditions.

A person never really gets over the anxiety. After years of enduring social events, it gets easier to hide those feelings and calm your nerves. It also helps that early on, social media was my platform of choice, doing written interviews and all sorts of obligations to promote my writing, my books—doing all that I could to be an artist and writer, except I wasn't doing everything I could. I hadn't given a single reading. Never spoke in front of a literary audience to promote a book of mine. And I had already put out six, going on seven.

This was 2014, and I moved to New York City to work in publishing. To try my hand at making it, just like so many others did. Hit the ground running; yeah, why not? Soon everywhere I looked, there was social pressure. I had to do something. I couldn't just hide in my cramped tiny Brooklyn bedroom. With all the literary ambition, I lost sight of many things, but one area that never fell into obscurity for me was heavy metal. I always adored the diverse range of aggressive vocals from bands like Suicide Silence and Whitechapel. Their vocalists, the late Mitch Lucker and Phil Bozeman, became mythical in my mind. I would imagine being them onstage doing all those vocals. If I had any confidence, I would have admitted that I could do their vocals. Jesus Christ, I certainly had enough lonely hours in the bedroom practicing against stereo playback.

In Greenpoint, a predominantly Polish neighborhood in Brooklyn, there's a metal bar called Saint Vitus. A dive bar perfect for someone like me. Dark and dank, most nights there are punk, hardcore, and metal concerts booked for the small, intimate room in the back. The booze is relatively cheap; the bartenders are chill enough that they won't chat you up unless you look like you need to talk it out. I am there on a Saturday night with a writer friend, both of us talking through the usual array of questions about our own writing, until they excuse themselves to use the restroom. The bartender must have seen that flicker of sadness, noticing just how much energy the entire encounter was sapping from me. "You good?" A shot on the house helps. "Yeah, just tired." He nods, pointing to the back room. "Wake up, things are picking up." Curiosity can just as easily pull you from the demons in your closet. It doesn't always end in failure. "What's going on?" He pours another shot. "Free shots if you can sing metal." My writer friend slides back into their seat, eavesdropping on the conversation. Go figure they remembered some of my Facebook posts about being in metal bands. "You should. It's a blast. I'm going on once my shift's over." The bartender encourages me to do it. Backed in the corner, like Ryu during the final round, and like Ryu, I was falling for the bait. But I wasn't going to get knocked out by the act.

I performed a Suicide Silence track that night called "Unanswered." To perhaps anyone else, it was mere drunken fun, but for me, it was a revelation, so euphoric it snapped something in my brain. Saint Vitus's metal karaoke was like going to therapy. Soon I was forcing myself to do readings. I can't confidently state that I don't still get nervous before speaking in public, but I can say with confidence that I no longer have full-blown panic attacks. There are no more dry heaves, spinning rooms, and locked closets with me curled up into a ball. No more doom scenarios playing out in my mind for weeks before and after the planned event. Gone are the manufactured beliefs that people hate me because I flaked on an obligation or stopped talking to them because getting any closer might mean having to "come out of my shell" and go with them to socially-nerve-racking events like weddings, dances, or worse, clubs where I would be forced to speak up. All the stillborn fear about myself, it is still a constant battle working through it, undoing the anxiety. However, seeing all the art that enters life at any given moment in so many ways does help put things into perspective. People aren't alone in feeling sad, suffering from the despondency of depression. If art teaches us anything, it's that nobody alive, and I mean *really* alive, isn't battling a closet of demons. It's too easy to hide.

Instead, I choose to scream. Who cares if I might lose a round or two? I prefer to drone all that sadness out with a wall of sound.

5 A ROLLERCOASTER OF EMOTIONS

All the cool kids ride the rollercoasters. They ride them fearlessly, the mere act of being launched into high-speed turns and drops a demonstration of their confidence. At least from my impressionable sixth or seventh grade eyes, the kids that got in line without even second-guessing were the loudest ones, often screaming at the top of their lungs about how wild and crazy the experience was going to be. I wanted to be one of them, too. Perhaps one of the only things I didn't fear were the zero-Gs and frenetic speed of a thrill ride. I learned to fear them much later when I was already too busy battling new social pressures in college.

One of our Spring class field trips was a visit to King's Dominion in Doswell, VA. Though local, the theme park had developed a reputation among thrill seekers (especially rollercoaster aficionados) due to the number of rides offered. Though no Cedar Point, King's Dominion built its reputation on big mainstays like Grizzly, the classic wooden coaster, Anaconda, with its hairpin turns, and the now-dismantled

Hypersonic XLC, which featured a straight 90 degree drop and 0 to 80MPH in 1.8 seconds. The latter coaster was so intimidating it would take me another year to finally give it a shot.

Everyone's excited because the moment we get to the park, it's clear that the whole place is ours. There are only two other classes for this slow Tuesday. King's Dominion publicity dubbed it a "senior graduation" celebration. All eighth-grade classes with only a couple weeks left before graduation are invited at a reduced admissions price for a day in the park. Walking down main street, I know this park well. 1999, nearly the millennium. Everything feels like the end. Everything feels like a new era. My first ride on Volcano, the back-to-back rides on Shockwave, the standing coaster where I finally caught the rollercoaster "bug." I couldn't get enough.

That morning when the class filed in people started dividing up into groups. I ended up as one of the cool kids, the four of us that wanted to go ride all the rollercoasters and high-intensity attractions. Chaperones were assigned to guide groups but keep a safe distance. We didn't even need to really fight over who made it into our group. Most of the class wanted to chat, walk around, maybe grab some cotton candy, maybe attempt to steal a beer. Nobody in my group seemed to notice, but I did. We had the entire park plotted for thrills. First up, the behemoth. The big one. Hypersonic XLC was all over TV, the commercial showing up frequently enough to wedge awareness deep into my consciousness. The 90-degree drop. The 80MPH speeds.

This was it, and because we were there early, on that special graduation celebration day, we were the only four queuing up for the ride. "Damn, nobody's here. That might be an omen," said some kid named Scott that I didn't really get along with. We didn't fight, but we also orbited different circles. He was more of a jock; I was a straight-up shy, withdrawn nerd in most cases except that day at King's Dominion. "It's because people are just getting into the park. Let's get the inaugural ride!" I led the way, the others giving in even if they had a moment of doubt. The operator and crew made sure we were safely strapped in. Scott already screaming, "Holy shit man," said Jesse, who sat next to me. We kept repeating the phrase, "This is crazy. This is crazy. This is crazy." Sixteen seconds later, the ride was over. Done. Like being hit by a truck, I stumbled out of the ride, craned my neck up at its 90-degree peak, and said, "Let's go again!"

Hypersonic XLC remains one of my most memorable coaster experiences because of the emotions that I went through as I waited in line, got closer to the front, and ended up going through with the ride. By the time I exited the ride, a little rattled but ultimately feeling weightless and euphoric, you could say I was addicted. There wasn't a rollercoaster I wouldn't ride. I rode it three more times that day and though my first was exclusively mine and my classmates to enjoy, the coaster became popular enough as the day at the park rolled on.

People saw these experiences as tests of courage. Really, it involves a bit of courage and a whole lot of surrender. When you get on that coaster, you're handing over trust and control of your wellbeing to the machine and its conductor about to send you on a journey.

"Thrill rides offer a unique type of scary experience," Margee Kerr writes in her book, *Scream: Chilling Adventures in the Science of Fear.* The rollercoaster is such a quick and frenetic experience that it effectively shuts off a person's ability to consciously think while enduring its duration, typically only a handful of minutes. We don't so much as ride the rollercoaster as much as we get strapped in and are shocked into an elevated consciousness. It's in this same elevated or suspended state that someone's amygdala could be triggered, resulting in the same fight-or-flight response at the apex of fear. But there's nowhere to go. You're along for the ride.

Jesse sits next to me throughout that inaugural ride on the Hypersonic XLC. The rollercoaster experience only lasts 30 or so seconds, which is nearly the same amount of time it takes for the ride's unique compressed air launch technology to prep up. "This is crazy." Even with all the ambient noise from the coaster itself, I can hear the panic in Jesse's voice. He's breathing in deep, with punctuated exhales, trademark characteristics of a panic attack. I have those often, and I know what that feels like, but in those seconds, I'm calm, observing my friend as he battles the fight or flight response, panic turning to fear as the ride reaches the pinnacle, that moment right before everyone strapped in knows it's time—go for launch. Through the sound barrier, pushing 0-to-80 in 1.8, Jesse speeds through fear by way of surprise. I hear him laughing, nothing coherent. As we reach that 90-degree drop, I'm feeling it too, but Jesse is screaming at the top of his lungs. If there could be any punctuation added to his scream, it would be a positive exclamation. We stare down the abyss, the intimidating drop pulling us in before we can take another breath. And then it's over, but the mind is still a few seconds behind. We sit there until the straps come off, reaping those moments cleansed by sheer surprise.

The emotional response we have with rollercoasters doesn't just come from anywhere. Like anything rooted in terror, we get off on the surprise and survival of that experience because perhaps we had more trouble and less success surviving past experiences and their subsequent traumas. In many ways, we're still working on surviving our trauma.

A person lays prone on a thin mattress, a pillow wedged under their neck for additional back support. It doesn't matter who this is, because it could be anyone. This is about surrendering and reopening those doors of the mind (and memory) that have been closed during our normal everyday lives. This person is alone with a therapist who oversees the session. Very little is said, at least at first. Eventually, the patient speaks up, but the therapist takes special care to take up as little space as possible. The patient swells in both speech and tears, a solemn cry building into panicked sobs. A few tremors and body twitches, the patient's face glowing red. The therapist listens intently

while making notes, being careful to say very little. "Mmm."
Eventually, the patient starts spasming again, more violently.
The cries are replaced with a diverse and borderline disturbing
wave of screams and guttural tremors. It's emotionally
exhausting, the therapist continuing the session as though
none of these horrible sounds and occurrences are transpiring.
By the end of the session, the patient returns to normal and
notices a difference. Maybe minor, but the world after a session
of primal therapy feels weightless, almost dizzying.

Primal therapy focuses trauma against the landscape of our past. Created by psychotherapist Arthur Janov to address issues with neurosis and psychological disrepair. He was widely outspoken in his work, especially in his book, *The Primal Scream*. The idea is to release repressed pain from childhood and teenage trauma by crying and throwing tantrums, essentially turning all that is deep and emotional into something physical. The most extreme are extended primal screams, pulling out an array of pain from the subconscious. It's scream therapy, basically.

"We have found a way into those early emotional archives and have learned to have access to those memories," wrote Janov. "Dredge them up from the unconscious, allowing us to re-experience them in the present, integrate them and no longer be driven by the unconscious." It's intense and controversial, to say the least. Janov claims that by pulling the pain into the conscious, we have more access to our feelings. They are no longer hidden away. and by having easier access to them, we might be able to face them head-on more effectively.

The therapy is popular, and it's not difficult to see why. It makes for a good headline, and an even better media story (especially when celebrities like Kim Kardashian and Kanye West talk about using primal therapy in interviews).

GPS led me to Williamsburg, just off the L. Easy enough, a few blocks, a 5-minute walk. The therapist's name is Glory, and her "office" is on the ground floor of a three-story residential building. "I do this on the side," she tells me. I wasn't passing any judgment. She must get it all the time, people second-guessing their appointment when they see it's a less professional affair. We sit opposite each other on the floor. "Let's get comfortable, shall we?" I'm on a large pillow while she is cross-legged on the floor. After a few minutes of discussion, she stops and doesn't so much as stare as much as she looks through me. It's a signal that we can begin. I don't know what to do, so I anxiously clear my throat, "So we just go into things or?" She doesn't make any facial expressions. A mere, "We go into things, hmm." It triggers me into thinking about the many times I would end up penalized by my mom for things I didn't mean to say. Things I didn't say, but because she had a way of teasing out the semantics of any phrase, I would end up being in the wrong, made wrong because she was the superior parent scolding a child. I talk about this and then find myself a little more worked up than usual, probably because Glory's staring at me.

"It's bullshit," I say. She repeats it, "It's bullshit." Looking around the room like I'm trying to find the source of an echo, I nod, "Yeah!" I repeat it, but this time I'm shouting. "Fucking bullshit!" Soon I'm using fewer words to voice my many frustrations. In warrior pose, I can feel the deep shouts resonating from my stomach. Glory says something like, "If only we could let it go." And it's in how she says it that causes my eyes to well up. Years of trying to hide my emotions—can't be too expressive, or else I won't be masculine enough—produces the opposite effect. I scream out once, twice. I almost wish she would scream along with me. That signals something within to snap free, and the tears pour down my face finally, and between gasps, I'm screaming full volume even though it hurts, even though I know I'm screaming from the throat, screaming wrong. I'm too far in to think I'm doing anything, much less if it's right or wrong. After the session, she gives me 15 minutes to get myself together. "Want some tea, or coffee? Maybe some water?" I can't help but feel like something has been stolen from me.

Screaming as an act of therapy is all around us. It doesn't take much to scream, merely a need for release. After my lone session of primal therapy, I felt noticeably lighter, but it wasn't because I had her with me as a guide. My therapist was essentially there in the event that something went wrong. But I felt the same feeling of weightlessness, the same heightening of the physical, along with the muting of my own never-ending internal monologue—I experienced the same thing on a rollercoaster. Primal therapy works for some people, and it has been trendy in some celebrity circles, but I found myself looking for my own meaning to what I cherish and trust most. I looked for choices in popular culture. You don't have to look very far. I found it early in thrill seeking by way of rollercoasters.

Later on, I found it in heavy metal and hardcore, performing practiced but no less cathartic vocal work. But there are so many options to be found across cultures. On April 24th, 2021, a gathering of institutions called the day "scream day," 24-hours in celebrating the awareness for just how positive and healthy a scream can be for your mental health.

The site promotes screaming in your car, in the woods, in your bathroom, anywhere you can safely let it all out without negatively surprising someone else. They even offered people to record their screams and post on Instagram, tagging @scream.day in hopes of being featured in their highlight reel. And if something like that isn't enough to prove that the opportunities are endless, how about a scream hotline? Chris Gollmar, an elementary school teacher, set up a hotline at the beginning of the COVID-19 lockdown, encouraging anyone to scream into the void. Literally. Just call in and scream. The awareness that your scream is being heard by someone else might help. It's certainly encouraging.

I do wonder how many actually did call in. Perhaps it became as addictive as primal therapy or screaming on a rollercoaster. Roller coasters, too, are a form of primal therapy within the context of a public experience where everyone involved can collectively address whatever they have bottled up inside, directed outward by way of surprise. Let it out. Scream. The person next to you could be screaming in fear while the one behind you is screaming bloody murder using all the pent-up animosity they have been battling over the last month due to a toxic work environment. You could be screaming in ecstasy, enjoying the moment fully as nostalgia from past coaster rides rush throughout your memory.

My lone experience with primal therapy isn't enough to pass judgment. Since the start of this book, I have thought about returning to Glory, maybe opting for the recommended allotment of sessions. It took months to come to grips with why I pushed away the thought, preferring to find it on my own. I'm stubborn by nature, rebellious to the point of self-destruction.

Thinking about going back, I can still feel the disappointment and shock that I experienced the last time I rode a rollercoaster. My addiction to thrill rides outlasted my adolescence, but I stopped going when life started asking more of me—more responsibilities, more worries, more pressures—and college semesters kept me laser-focused on things happening on campus.

"That tiny thing?" Crystal and I are on a vacation, spring break, celebrating four months of our relationship. Still in the honeymoon phase, we can't take our minds or bodies off each other. I spend money I don't have setting up a week long road

trip jutting north from Orlando, Florida to North and South Carolina, hoping to get some hikes and camping in. Neither of us are much into nature though. Most of the trip consists of Airbnbs, going to bars, and then drunkenly spending time together back at the rental. But we do manage to get out sometimes.

We notice a local carnival while staying at an Airbnb just outside Atlanta. "It could be fun?" Crystal sounds skeptical. I'm feeling a little restless. The day got off on the wrong foot, our first fight. Not much of one really. But we bickered a little, which put added pressure on us to entertain each other, trying our best to hide what we were really thinking: Uh oh. Is this a crack? Hairline perhaps, but still, would this relationship hold if it couldn't even handle a simple tiny aimless road trip?

The carnival had the usual suspects—merry-go-round, hall of mirrors, parlor games—but there was something else, too. The lone surprise. Prime real estate. A traveling rollercoaster that didn't even have a name. Crystal notices my eyes light up and grabs my hand, sauntering up to the coaster with no line. Everything's fine until we're strapped in, and the same comforts, the relinquishing of control from before, kicks in. This time, instead of calm, I feel chaos. My heart beats rapidly, my throat growing dry. "What's wrong?" Crystal being there doesn't help. The coaster kicks in, rattling across the track like the car might fall off at any moment. It does nothing to help me leave my mind. Instead of the brain ceasing its internal monologue, the ride somehow magnifies my anxiety. "We could fly off this fucker." That's all I could think about.

The less restrained a person, the more likely they'll be able to enjoy the ride. "As we age, however, so does our vestibular system, making it harder to find our balance," Kerr explains. "The loss of control and disorientation can also be hard to tolerate in adulthood."

At age 22, I had grown and changed as a person. I had become an adult. In the years since my stint of rollercoaster addiction, I had found that shock and awe, that surrender, in music, art, and other people, like Crystal. Maybe there's something to primal therapy. I should try it again. We're searching for ways to understand ourselves and our trauma. I guess what surprises me the most is just how much goes into the object of screaming and how while what we release might shock and surprise, it's on the brink of vocal impact that we feel alive.

We could all stand to scream out without worrying about being judged.

6 OMG I'M SCREAMING

The internet is loud, like *really* loud. You could be in a heated argument or getting dragged on Twitter, but from a distance, you're typing or thumbing through digital space, physically voiceless and mentally somewhere else. We have the world in the palm of our hands, and with it comes the pressure. I joined Facebook in 2011, Twitter in 2013, and Instagram in 2015. Before those, Myspace, LiveJournal, and even AOL Instant Messenger ran through my veins. Those felt different, though. It wasn't until Facebook and Twitter bled into every waking moment that I began to experience the feeling of needing to document everything that happens in my life to ensure that it added "meaning" to my actions and decisions. It wasn't a conscious decision. By tweeting and posting, commenting and taking part in the discourse, I found myself becoming another voice shouting and screaming for validation through the dozens, sometimes hundreds of tweets and posts I add to the swirling chaos of social media.

When you scream and someone screams back, the validation is bliss, and that bliss is infectious. It didn't take long for me to adhere to the daily grind of being active and "living online." Everything I did was mined for content—a good, buzzy tweet, a thirsty or envious photo for Instagram. Everything I experienced had an additional filter of dire need.

I couldn't just live in the moment. This folded into my own ambitions as a writer. Though I worked hard, my attention was always split between social media and everything else. The volume of my tweets became louder, and with that loudness, the validation and addiction increased in demand.

After so many years of living online with the would-be encouragement of my followers, I decided to do something drastic, moving the documentation of the moment to the point of an avatar or reality television contestant.

I'm going on a cross-country road trip, directed/guided by social media, & writing a book abt it. #FollowMeBook http:// bit.ly/2pFNbff

That was the announcement tweeted out on May 12th, 2017. By June 1st, I was on the road, everything I did turning into some sort of content online. One month. One whole month to chase whatever it was that I was chasing. At the time, I wouldn't have dared admit that I was chasing the same thing from the beginning: validation. The difference now was that my social media obsession had merged with my writing process. I was screaming for career success so loudly that I pushed some people away. I was too loud, too earnest, my content borderline suffocating like the most frightening, surprising, or disgusting bellows.

There was no book. It wasn't for lack of trying; the book, tentatively titled *Follow Me*, never got past the proposal stage. A few chapters and an attempt by an agent that saw the project purely from an opportunity level, not much else. The failure had its effect on me. To this day, I still get pains in my upper back and neck whenever I get a notification. Whenever I see people rushing to get their hot takes in on a subject that routinely has little to do with them, I feel nauseous. Then—because I no longer have it in me to engage in the discourse—because I'm not involved, I feel even sicker, dizzy and borderline violently ill.

First, someone tweets, and it's a tweet that errs too informal, with undertones of annoyance peppering its 280 characters. "I'm adding to a pretty insufferable discourse but it's weird to me when people act like Catcher in the Rye *is about a shitty 25-year-old guy they dated in 2009 and not like, a 16-year-old who is having a hard time handling the death of his little brother."*

*And then it gets some likes, a few retweets. People react. And then people tweet in reply. "'*Catcher in the Rye *is bad, actually' is just such a phenomenally uninteresting take for uninteresting people trying far too hard to prove otherwise. Real 'baby's first opinion' type shit." And then that reply gets attention.*

The term itself, going viral, sounds like a joke. But this is no joke. People react. They reply. Many are angry. Most a person could argue, are on the verge of shouting. "Well if it's so great, then the fact that SO many people really hate it is an indictment of our education system." We're only just getting started. Twitter's algorithm parses this discussion and adds it to its What's Happening (trending news) column for anyone even remotely seeking literary or book topics. Then more people see it. More people react. The replies add up. The original tweet becomes coveted and tossed around like a t-shirt whose slogan lasts, at best, a flash during the heat of summer.

Seeing this happen, I want to scream. It's all so excruciating! That's partly why I went to Glory. Maybe I should try primal therapy again. For now, I'm writing it out here because in all that social media obsession, social media road trip, social media clout chasing, social media discourse, there was one area that I could leave behind, at least in terms of emotional involvement. Social media could be just that, a utility from which you can check-in and then check out. Learning still to this day, I can hear other people screaming for attention. It's louder than I ever expected.

I guess I really was that excruciating. Thank you to anyone that tolerated and, dare I say it, engaged with me all those years.

You no longer need to vocally scream to scream. We've advanced our social technologies to the point of gut response, zero forethought. Two steps forward, three steps back.

One person DMs (direct messages) the other on Facebook. "Hey." Both are friends IRL but use Messenger because they believe it's quicker when really, it's because they started talking in the first place on the app, and it has since become an essential component of their friendship. "Yo." There is seldom any impetus to a conversation. They could talk about anything. Most of the time, one is bored at work, in their cubicle, suffering through the doldrums of the day. The other is chatting in between clients, a personal trainer hustling to make ends meet at Planet Fitness. "So you know that fucker, Blue Shirt, from the Russian Circles show last month?" Of course they remember—Blue Shirt is the name given to someone that nearly got into a fight with the personal trainer. Beer and post-metal and some pent-up end-of-the-work week aggression and personal trainer got a little confrontational. Blue Shirt was the one that reciprocated. "Yeah, guy was a dick. What about?" The friend gets a thrill out of being able to spread the news. "Get this. Turns out Blue Shirt is the guitarist from the opener." That gets personal trainer's attention. "Really?" The other is replying in seconds, a string of emojis. Personal trainer stands at one of the abdominal machines, idly staring at his phone, fingers tapping against the screen. He exhales, expressionlessly types, "OMG I'm screaming."

We can write what we feel without expressing it physically. I'm doing that right now. Yet we fail to remember that even the most powerful physical registers of human expression, like the scream, can become purely invisible, funneled through technology and the internet. It can become metaphorical, stripped of its trademark bold first impression.

A quick skim of any social media platform, and you'll find word strings and emoji combinations. Marked throughout various comments, inquiries, and gestures of human thought are phrases that signify what we wouldn't dare express in the moment, not where we are remotely.

Internal screaming has become a common expression, with variations of the phrase, "I'm screaming," used commonly internet speak. The Twitter account @infinite_ scream tweets out, "AHHHHHHHHHHHHHHHHHHH" every 10-15 minutes nonstop, effectively screaming into the void. And then there's Twitch, where users explore the extremes of ASMR, just as often sending the dial of interest to an entirely different number—full-on noise and screams. It's much like what neuroscientist Luc Arnal and his colleagues, including David Poeppel, at the University of Geneva discovered during their study of the roughness of the scream: "If sound roughness is an effective feature for screams to constitute an alarm signal, it might also be exploited by man-made technological devices that generate non-biological acoustic signals to alert humans to danger."

On the internet, "screams" generate similar emotional responses, though the most common of them are disgust and anger. These actions often act like a mirror, projecting the same emotion onto the user.

The worst of it is when punctuation and capitalization come into play.

"While there's no actual yelling with voices involved, reading a sentence using only capital letters feels like

GETTING HIT IN THE FACE BY A VERY ANGRY PERSON," explained Rebecca Greenfield, former staff writer at *The Wire*. In an essay for *The Atlantic*, "The Art of Screaming Online," Greenfield mines those early impetuses for when internet speak and etiquette universally accepted when, where, and how a scream can be generated on the internet.

During the early days of the internet, when dial-up tortured everyone with its own mechanical wails, text styling—whether it was through multiple fonts, bold, italics, or caps-lock—was still novel, users doing whatever they thought resonated best with their message. AIM and chat rooms helped forge a style or standard of practice. Eventually, the block-like look of words all in caps, or worse, affected with additional stylistic flair, became a clear indication of cringe. Technological advancements and the advent of web 2.0 only accelerated these standards. Nowadays, it's not unheard of for someone to end up banned, fired, or outed for using ALL CAPS. "If a typist uses all capitals, it means the worst," noted Greenfield. There exists the opposite of ALL CAPS, which is a sort of an interpretation of toggle case: sOmEtHiNg LiKe ThIs. The opposite extreme is an insincere statement or chortle done in jest.

I AM SCREAMING. LISTEN TO ME. I'M SO ANGRY. WHY AM I STILL TYPING LIKE THIS? Sorry. So then, through natural evolution, I'M SCREAMING became a common language for the scream. It's quite alarming to note that the scream itself had similar origins, based on a need for expression during the primal days when language was limited. It became a more stylized and niche form of communication when survival was no longer a primary issue; human language became sophisticated enough that a fight was, and is, more likely to be verbal rather than physical. Now we've evolved with linguistic image iconographies, like emojis, to resemble the act of a scream while stripping the actual vocal register out of it. The roughness is there, the pitch too, embedded in the linguistic context.

A person has reason to go online. The news maybe, but they also have news themselves. Something to share, and it's exciting enough that they can barely contain themselves. They sign into Facebook, spending a few moments to check their notifications. When was the last time they signed in? Months, at least. A college friend got a new job. Colleague is pregnant. "Well good!" They say, but their actual response is a "CONGRATS." All caps, with a few heart emojis. In a few pages alone, the volume of good news is intoxicating. A person makes sure to like or "love" a post, and for those handfuls of friends, family, and colleagues, they offer up their congratulations. It's only fair, they think, knowing that they're about to do the same. But what if nobody reacts? What if it only gets like 40 likes? All these posts have upwards of 200. One of them broke a thousand. A person can get lost in such negative thoughts. Instead they write out what's on their mind. "I'm so excited to announce that I'm moving—to my dream city for my dream job!" All of it is true, but it isn't their dream job, not exactly. It's a good gig, an entry level marketing role at a clothing brand. The future opportunities could be great, though. The positive response rolls in, and soon enough, a person no longer worries about lack of a response. Someone they used to know really well messages them, "I'm so happy for you! I'm screaming!" A person reads such things and feels that warmth, but there's almost always a sense of doubt.

Though it's almost effortless to assume that a scream will always occupy the negative end of the emotional spectrum, the same rush can translate as a positive. That same thread of disgust has its exact opposite by way of users announcing their career moves or engagements, new kids or new moves, a book deal, or a deal booked for a brand-new home. People go online to share absolute cheer, making announcements and spreading impressions of their happiness. When they say *OMG I'm screaming*, they are signaling a flicker of performed emotional gratitude. Or, to put it simply, they are celebrating. They are celebrating because, dare I say it, they are happy.

Saturday afternoon. Two story house with a fenced in yard. Multiple picnic tables are draped in colorful tablecloths. Numerous plates with flavorful and flagrant foods are placed on top. Number of people in attendance must be around 25, all of them cheering and dancing in between sipping drinks or trying some of the food.

In the far-right corner, a mariachi band of five sing loudly, setting the cheery tone of the event. It's a celebration, not

*for anyone in particular but rather the fact that it's the first
time the family has been in one physical location for over a
decade. It also happens to be the 16th of September, Mexican
Independence Day. When the current song concludes, one
of the band members addresses the family in their native
language. Some look at each other, slightly bashful; most cheer
along, warming up their voices. The member addressing the
family engages the call and response. He lets out an infectious
cheer, and then so do members of the family. It's a crescendo
that might call the attention of their neighbors, who wonder,
with awe, what's going on? It sounds like fun. It's something
big. A celebration!*

On September 16th, 1810, Miguel Hidalgo y Costilla declared
a revolt against Spanish rule, starting the Mexican War of
Independence. Many commemorate these fateful moments
in history with a celebratory "grito," or a scream that typically
is used within celebrations, complete with mariachi music,
to express pure joy and pride. It's infectious, and should one
hear the grito, you might find yourself interpreting how to
also take part in the cheer.

In Austin, Texas, the call and response cry, known
as "Grito de Dolores," or the "Cry of Dolores," has been a
recognized celebration—September 16th—for 23 years.

The grito is merely one example of a scream taking on
both celebratory and cultural significance. When it's so
easy to use a scream to express anger, disgust, or sadness,
it's reassuring to remember that screaming out can be about

euphoria and pride, too. They scream because, well . . . they're HAPPY.

A weeknight. Maybe a Thursday. A young 27-year-old sits at his desk in his bedroom, one of three rooms in a Brooklyn apartment that he shares with another roommate. He works into the late evening, taking advantage of the quiet. His roommate is out, who knows where. A few productive hours working on some code for a personal project meets a sharp and sudden end when he hears the front door crash open, twin voices an outpour in the common room. They're loud, likely buzzed from a handful of drinks. Something's different about it, though, muffled speech and more sounds than anything really said. "Oh god," he sighs when he hears them. It's difficult not to imagine things vividly when all the right sounds are within earshot.

They're making out on the couch. He puts on his headphones, pushing the whole mental visual aside. When he needs to use the bathroom, he's startled to see that the apartment is lightless, his roommate's bedroom door locked, faint light visible from the crack under the door. Then he hears it: a masculine grunt, a feminine shout. A few moans combine into a blend of skin and sweat, eventually he can't help but feel awkward as he hears her climax, this woman he hasn't even met, screaming out with purity. The 27-year-old blinks and feels gross, "He could have told me he was bringing someone over." Barely a mutter. The damage is already imprinted into their mind.

Just because the scream is loud, it doesn't mean it's meant to lacerate. Research has suggested that a scream is nothing more than an attempt to call attention with a combination of powerful pitch and roughness and an equally resonant emotion. In a study published by *PLOS Biology*, it was discovered that of all the emotions in those screams, the ones that were made from joy, or ecstasy, were processed more quickly by the human listener. Joy is infectious and easy to identify. The human brain has evolved to better process a happy scream, positive stimuli, rather than the negative; it's almost as if we have grown as a society to keep an ear out for the celebration, wanting so much to be a part of it.

Survival these days is avoiding FOMO. Survival is not enacting the possibility of social suicide.

Not long after, I moved to the city. The sweltering heat of summer 2015. I spend most of it trying to fight off panic attacks and anxiety. This meant a lot of exploring the city on foot, meeting people I knew online in one-on-one hangouts at dive bars. The typical hour or so of chatting over 2 or 3 (or, for me, 4) drinks before returning to my cramped lofted bedroom to spend the rest of the night with my headphones on, listening to music and scouring the internet.

Another night meant yet another hangout, or "meet and greet," as I had started calling them by way of explaining to my two roommates, who were both far more sociable and clearly city people, out every night while I still tended to stay in my little closet of a room two or three times a week.

Just down the street, there was a bar and restaurant called Eastwick. We knew each other online, but not well. Acquaintances at best. The hour and 2 or 3 drinks ended up being 3 hours and a bar crawl. We had a good time, really hitting it off. Next time we did the same: multiple unplanned visits to bars, bookstores, and even a speakeasy in Manhattan.

Another time, we hang out on the rooftop; it was hot, too hot for clothes. It was there that the rules of attraction gave way to a kiss, a sweaty fondling, and an episode of heavy petting before we ended up back in my cramped closet of a room. My roommates were home. One was asleep. Our walls were thin; I knew this because they heard everything I did. I used to hear about it from them all the time. "What were you watching last night?" "Could you keep the music down? It's cool, I love Mastodon too, but not at 3AM when I'm trying to sleep." "You play videogames in there? Cool, I can't even afford them."

Naked on my lofted bed, every minor move resulting in the creaking of the wooden beams, I couldn't get remotely aroused. The night could have been a failure if the stroke and tender brush of her breast against my own bare chest wasn't such a turn-on. Soon we connected, and each gyration brought us into more of a rhythm. Mentally I was elsewhere; I never even got anywhere close to enjoying the moment because I was too busy listening to her breaths, and then her moans, worrying that she might wake up my roommate.

It's like *A Quiet Place*, but the monsters are my social anxiety. Screams of joy were denied, yet it wasn't so much that I didn't want what we were having. I simply couldn't separate possible judgment and nearby ears catching notice of what we were doing. I was too self-conscious, too busy thinking outwardly when really what we were doing was celebrating a connection. The very same connection that would last a year of our lives. We seldom get any second chances to know and care for someone; maybe it's worth letting out a scream of joy, a neck-turning jolt of ecstasy. So what? You're having sex. Better yet, you're *enjoying* sex. Why are those screams so embarrassing? Maybe they want to feel what you're feeling. It's a person alive, the scream once again confirmation of that life. Enough with the doubt and self-judgement. Stop self-judging the sounds you make. I say it to myself, and I tell it to you, all of you that feel self-conscious when you're feeling great and fear letting out a scream of joy. Let emotions be emotions, just as facts are facts. *OMG I'm screaming*, and it feels so good.

Go ahead and be loud.

EPILOGUE

THE BODY

He had a great time. Last night was wild. Up until 3AM, bar crawl with a few friends he hasn't seen since COVID-19, the lockdown, and the would-be end of the world. Last night things felt new, almost the same. It was there that he caught up with Jeff and Macy and Andrew and John and Dan. Everyone had experienced something drastic and new. Voices on top of voices, excitingly retelling a year's worth of self-improvement and self-inspection. He can hear it in his voice, feeling the pull in his throat. Between laughter, he chats about finishing a book and starting a proposal, working from home helping with getting back in shape. There's talk about a breakup. People lighten the conversation by layering it with jokes. He laughs really hard. The laughter continues as the conversation falls into that ebb and flow that happens as people get comfortable (meaning buzzed). A few rounds at Washington Commons, then it's time to walk down the street to Fulton Grand. There's a block party down the street, making it loud even though they're sitting outside. He shouts whole lines from a poem that he claims defined his 2020. There was another bar after that, but he forgets the name. A heart to heart with Macy, who you always had a crush on. At some point, he forgets the chain of events, but it ends in his building's backyard with John and Dan; everyone else has long since parted ways. The three eat late night Popeyes chicken sandwiches while sipping from a "nightcap" bottle. He doesn't remember what happens but one thing's for sure: He had a great time.

One of the worst things that can happen to a person is losing their voice. When you do lose it, the effect is incredibly debilitating and often painful. During our resting state, when aren't speaking, the vocal folds are lax and open so that we can breathe. Upon speaking, they snap together, the faintest amount of air pushing through the tiny space between the clenched folds.

A throat strained from overuse is the breathy, raspy, and otherwise scratchy condition of being hoarse. The medical term is laryngitis, the inflammation of the larynx. It might feel minor, or it might feel like you've swallowed razor blades. The vocal folds are built to handle an excess of tension; it's a muscle, after all. However, when the soft tissues in the throat rub and bang against each other to the point of irritation or tearing, the larynx becomes compromised, and you end up muted, limited in speech. "Human throats, no matter how well-oiled, can't take the stress of screaming," Elena Passarello wrote in her book, *Let Me Clear My Throat.*

We've evolved to rely on language and voice. Yet the muscles in our throats still contain that essential fragility, which is an uncanny metaphor for the scream itself—powerful and versatile but underneath it's all depth and vulnerable feeling.

Maybe you did strain it from overuse, too much elevated chatter, and too much alcohol leading to the overextension; the throat needs time to heal after heavy use. Laryngitis typically lasts about a week. The body is great like that—it heals itself from wounds and injuries. However, as we age, things change. Our bodies don't always heal back to normal; our voices adopt the decades, our memories and experiences forming the luster in every vowel.

People begin to "sound old," at different times. It typically begins in your 50s, though some may still carry a full voice reminiscent of their twenties long into their 60s or 70s. Through atrophy of the vocal folds, thinning of the mucus membranes, and stiffening of the connective tissues, a voice evolves into the age of the body that carries it, and so too does the sounds it manages to produce.

Your deathbed will be different from mine, but there you are. There we are, bodies motionless, laying still. A condition or affliction contributing to our journey to the end—it could be cancerous, an accident; it could be anything, and it's guaranteed that it'll be uniquely yours.

Death may come for everyone, but how it finds you is a lot like when you attempt to scream out for a nurse, for a loved one sitting nearby, but you can't. You hear only the roughness, the hissing of a rattle. Near, so very near. Everyone knows. But you don't know because you're still trying to speak. You're still trying to scream and shout. There's still so much to tell people; so much has happened during all these years, maybe you could hand over some advice. Or maybe you just don't want to die alone. How do we go? How do we leave this body, this earth? How do we leave this life behind? Eventually, it happens, there is no how or why, but in those dying moments, you can see the rise and fall of your chest slow down, feel the dryness of your vocal folds and the heaviness of your eyelids. Tired, so very tired, there must be some specific moment when you turn, when we go from alive to being dead. The flatline, yes, but in the body, you are still alive until it gives out—the heart and soul loosening their grip on the body finally and saying, Okay, *let's go.*

Before the death rattle, we exhale one last time. Then, the death rattle will arrive; you'll hear it in those final moments, as brittle as the body generating the sound. Though a person might cry out, at death's door, a scream is only half of itself, revealing its emotional depth without its full sound. A scream is a command, a call for attention, and most of all, an act of survival. In a scream, we express our feelings, transcending any language barrier. Whether fear, anger, disgust, surprise, or happiness, we feel it, and it can be found in a scream.

The first thing we do when we're born is scream out in surprise, unaware until the moment we exist that existence was such a thing. How poetic then that the last thing we do as we die is give into the silence.

The body gives out, but the hope is that you never gave in. You may go hoarse, the side-effects of expressing yourself, but never, *ever*, lose your voice.

REFERENCES

Prologue – The Voice

"Call." *English Synonyms and Antonyms: With Notes on the Correct Use of Prepositions*, by James Champlin Fernald, Funk & Wagnall, 2010.

Fellbaum, C., & Miller, G. A. (1990). Folk psychology or semantic entailment? Comment on Rips and Conrad (1989). Psychological Review, 97(4), 565–570. https://doi.org/10.1037 /0033-295X.97.4.565

Chapter 1 – A Scream in the Night

"Chapter 12: Surprise, Astonishment, Fear, Horror." The Expression of the Emotions in Man and Animals, by Charles Darwin, Appleton & Company, 1872.

"Fight or Flight: The Science of Fear . . . And Why We Like Scary Movies." University of Pennsylvania Health System, 2 Oct. 2017. www.pennmedicine.org/updates/blogs/health-and -wellness/2017/october/fear.

Geaghan-Breiner, Meredith, and Hailey Gavin. "Professional Acting Coach Reviews Iconic Screams in Horror Movies." *Insider*, 22 July 2020, www.insider.com/acting-coach-reviews -iconic-screams-in-horror-movies-2020-5.

Hutchinson, Sean. "What Is the Wilhelm Scream?" *Mental Floss*, 16 Aug. 2018, www.mentalfloss.com/article/60236/where-did -wilhelm-scream-come-and-why-do-so-many-filmmakers-use -it.

Moyer, Nancy. "Amygdala Hijack: When Emotion Takes Over." *Healthline*, 21 Sept. 2021. www.healthline.com/health/stress/ amygdala-hijack.

Nava, Fabrizio. "Top Bone Chilling Horror Movie Screams." *DoYouRemember?*, 2015, doyouremember.com/357/top-bone -chilling-horror-movie-screams.

Passarello, Elena. *Let Me Clear My Throat: Essays*. Sarabande Books, 2012.

Rochon, Debbie. "The Legend of the Scream Queen." *GC Magazine*. Archived from the original on 13 Aug. 2007.

Ryzik, Melena. "They Scream! We Scream!" The New York Times, The New York Times, 9 Oct. 2020, www.nytimes.com/2020/10 /29/movies/scream-horror.html.

Chapter 2 – Stand and Deliver

Arnal, Luc H., et al. "Human Screams Occupy a Privileged Niche in the Communication Soundscape." *Current Biology*, vol. 25, no. 15, 3 Aug. 2015, doi:https://doi.org/10.1016/j. cub.2015.06.043.

"The Evolution of Screaming." YouTube, uploaded by The Punk Rock MBA, 22 Sept 2020, https://youtu.be/si-tcjj7L3U

Lapidos, Juliet. "How Mean Are Drill Sergeants?". *Slate*, 22 Sept 2009, https://slate.com/news-and-politics/2009/09/how-mean-are-drill-sergeants-in-real-life.html

Mao, Zedong. *Selected Works of Mao Tse-Tung*. Oxford: Pergamon Press, 1961. Print.

McAndrew, Frank T. "Why we love big, blood-curdling screams." *The Conversation*, 28 Oct 2019, https://theconversation.com/why-we-love-big-blood-curdling-screams-124148

McKay, Brett & Kate. "Sound Your Barbaric Yawp! 20 Battle Cries Through the Ages." *The Art of Manliness*, 8 June 2015, https://www.artofmanliness.com/articles/battle-cries/

Whyte, Chelsea. "Aaaaaargh! The true nature of screaming has finally been revealed." *The New Scientist*, 18 May 2019, https://www.newscientist.com/article/2203197-aaaaaargh-the-true-nature-of-screaming-has-finally-been-revealed/

Williams, Sarah P. "Why screams are so scary." *Science*, 16 July 2015, https://www.science.org/content/article/why-screams-are-so-scary-rev2

Chapter 3 – Step Forward, Speak Up

Bryan, Candace. "The Soothing Power of Protests, And Why You Should Scream, Shout and Let It All Out There." *Cosmopolitan*, 13 Jan 2017, https://www.cosmopolitan.com/politics/a8655821/protest-hard-scream-loudly/

Cohen, Elliot D. "Can Screaming or Yelling Be Bad for Your Relationship?" *Psychology Today*, 17 Aug. 2015, www.psychologytoday.com/us/blog/what-would-aristotle-do/201508/can-screaming-or-yelling-be-bad-your-relationship.

Crowley, James. "Man Who Went Viral for Screaming at Capitol Rioters Says He 'Needed to Let Them Have It.'" *Newsweek*, 8 Jan 2021, https://www.newsweek.com/who-guy-porch-viral-video-yelling-protesters-1560103

Groopman, Jerome. "The Anatomy of Hope." *The New York Times*, 22 Feb 2004, https://www.nytimes.com/2004/02/22/books/chapters/the-anatomy-of-hope.html

"Polish-Belarusian activist Jana Shostak talks about her protest." *Polish News*, 24 May 2021, https://polishnews.co.uk/polish-belarusian-activist-jana-shostak-talks-about-her-protest/

"Screaming artist electrifies Belarus protests in Warsaw." *France 24*, 6 Nov 2021, https://www.france24.com/en/live-news/20210611-screaming-artist-electrifies-belarus-protests-in-warsaw

Chapter 4 – I Have No Mouth, and I Must Scream

Abramović, Marina. "Freeing the Voice." 1975. https://www.youtube.com/watch?v=pBVzJI6m72A

"Let It All Out! The Art of Screaming." *Elephant*, 22 Aug 2018, https://elephant.art/let-art-screaming/

Rutledge, David. "Monotony and the sacred: a brief history of drone music." *ABC*, 6 May 2015, https://www.abc.net.au/radionational/programs/earshot/monotony-and-the-sacred/6448906

Sooke, Alastair. "What is the meaning of The Scream?" *BBC*, 3 Mar 2016, https://www.bbc.com/culture/article/20160303-what-is-the-meaning-of-the-scream

Chapter 5 – A Rollercoaster of Emotions

Janov, Arthur. *New Primal Scream*. Abacus, 1991.

Kerr, Margee. *Scream: Chilling Adventures in the Science of Fear*. PublicAffairs, 2017.

Oliver, Rae. "Scream Therapy: 5 Reasons Why Screaming Is Good For You." *Truly Experiences*, 4 Nov 2020, https://trulyexperiences.com/blog/why-screaming-good-for-you/

Stephens, Richard. "The psychology of roller coasters." *The Conversation*, 11 July 2018, https://theconversation.com/the-psychology-of-roller-coasters-99166

Chapter 6 – OMG I'm Screaming

Chamary, JV. "Are Humans More Sensitive To Screams From Sex Than Fear?". *Forbes*, 14 Apr. 2021, https://www.forbes.com/sites/jvchamary/2021/04/14/science-human-screams/?sh=1d3464582fc2

Fink, Kimmie. "An Elementary Teacher Designed a 'Call in and Scream' Hotline Because of Course They Did." *We Are Teachers*, 19 Jan 2021, https://www.weareteachers.com/just-scream-hotline/

Frühholz S, Dietziker J, Staib M, Trost W (2021). "Neurocognitive processing efficiency for discriminating human non-alarm rather than alarm scream calls." *PLoS Biol* 19(4): e3000751. https://doi.org/10.1371/journal.pbio.3000751

Greenfeld, Rebecca. "The Art of Screaming Online." *The Atlantic*, 13 June 2013, https://www.theatlantic.com/technology/archive/2013/06/art-screaming-online/314295/

Kiefer, Philip. "Our most recognizable screams are the most joyful." *Popular Science*, 15 Apr 2021, https://www.popsci.com/story/science/human-scream-study/

Epilogue – The Body

"Hoarseness." National Institute of Deafness and Other Communication Disorders, U.S. Department of Health and Human Services, www.nidcd.nih.gov/health/hoarseness.

INDEX

OBJECTLESSONS

Cross them all off your list.

9781501358159

9781501353277

9781501348716

9781501353024

9781501344350

9781501361906

"Perfect for slipping in a pocket and pulling out when life is on hold."

– Toronto Star

bird
ERIK ANDERSON
BLOOMSBURY

9781501353352

cell tower
STEVEN E. JONES
BLOOMSBURY

9781501348815

compact disc
ROBERT BARRY
BLOOMSBURY

9781501348518

ocean
STEVE MENTZ
BLOOMSBURY

9781501348631

high heel
SUMMER BRENNAN
BLOOMSBURY

9781501325991

hood
ALISON KINNEY
BLOOMSBURY

9781501307409

Blackface

Examines Hollywood's painful, enduring ties to racist performances"

—*Variety*

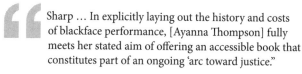

Sharp … In explicitly laying out the history and costs of blackface performance, [Ayanna Thompson] fully meets her stated aim of offering an accessible book that constitutes part of an ongoing 'arc toward justice."

—*Times Higher Education*

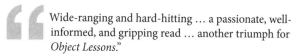

Wide-ranging and hard-hitting … a passionate, well-informed, and gripping read … another triumph for *Object Lessons*."

—*New York Journal of Books*

Sticker

> " Hoke (*The Groundhog Forever*) offers up an evocative reflection on queerness, race, and his hometown of Charlottesville, Va., in this conceptual 'memoir in 20 stickers.' Part of Bloomsbury's *Object Lessons* series, his book uses the humble sticker as a metaphorical linchpin for a series of essays that [offer] a unique perspective on one of the most infamous cities in recent American history."
>
> —*Publishers Weekly*

> " We're not entirely objective here, but we're quite fond of the *Object Lessons* series—and Henry Hoke's contribution might boast the most striking cover design the series has had to date. Hoke's book uses stickers to chronicle everything from queer identity to the recent history of Charlottesville, Virginia—all of which should make this a book that sticks with you long after you've read it. (Pun intended, oh yes.)"
>
> —*Volume I Brooklyn*

Spacecraft

It's a story born of a specific cultural imaginary common among children of the last decades of the previous century … *Spacecraft*, then, is a vehicle in which Morton meditates on futurality. The Millennium Falcon, along with hyperspace, is at the center of this meditation."

—*3 Quarks Daily*

Burger

Based on meticulous, and comprehensive, research, Adams has packed a stunning, gripping expose into these few pages – one that may make you rethink your relationship with this food. Five stars."

—*San Francisco Book Review*

Adams would seem the least likely person to write about hamburgers with her philosophically lurid antipathy to carnivory. But if the point is to deconstruct this iconic all-American meal, then she is the woman for the job."

—*Times Higher Education*

High Heel

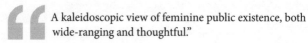

A kaleidoscopic view of feminine public existence, both wide-ranging and thoughtful."

—*Jezebel*

From Cinderella's glass slippers to Carrie Bradshaw's Manolo Blahniks, Summer Brennan deftly analyzes one of the world's most provocative and sexualized fashion accessories ... Whether you see high heels as empowering or a submission to patriarchal gender roles (or land somewhere in between), you'll likely never look at a pair the same way again after reading *High Heel*."

—*Longreads*

Brennan's book, written in very small sections, is short, but powerful enough to completely change your world view."

—*Refinery29*

Hood

Provocative and highly informative, Alison Kinney's *Hood* considers this seemingly neutral garment accessory and reveals it to be vexed by a long history of violence, from the Grim Reaper to the KKK and beyond-a history we would do well to address, and redress. Readers will never see hoods the same way again."

—Sister Helen Prejean, author of *Dead Man Walking*

Hood is searing. It describes the historical properties of the hood, but focuses on this object's modern-day connotations. Notably, it dissects the racial fear evoked by young black men in hoodies, as shown by the senseless killings of unarmed black males. It also touches on U.S. service members' use of hoods to mock and torture prisoners at Abu Ghraib. Hoods can represent the (sometimes toxic) power of secret affiliations, from monks to Ku Klux Klan members. And clearly they can also be used by those in power to dehumanize others. In short, *Hood* does an excellent job of unspooling the many faces of hoods."

—*Book Riot*

[*Hood*] is part of a series entitled Object Lessons, which looks at 'the hidden lives of ordinary things' and which are all utterly 'Fridge Brilliant' (defined by TV Tropes as an experience of sudden revelation, like the light coming on when you open a refrigerator door). ... In many ways *Hood* isn't about hoods at all. It's about what – and who – is under the hood. It's about the hooding, the hooders and the hoodees ... [and] identity, power and politics. ... Kinney's book certainly reveals the complex history of the hood in America."

—*London Review of Books*

Personal Stereo:

[Rebecca Tuhus-Dubrow's] thoughtfulness imbues this chronicle of a once-modern, now-obsolete device with a mindfulness that isn't often seen in writing about technology."

—*Pitchfork* (named one of *Pitchfork*'s favorite books of 2017)

After finishing *Personal Stereo*, I found myself wondering about the secret lives of every object around me, as if each device were whispering, 'Oh, I am much so more than meets the eye'... Tuhus-Dubrow is a master researcher and synthesizer. ... *Personal Stereo* is a joy to read."

—*Los Angeles Review of Books*

Souvenir

Rolf Potts writes with the soul of an explorer and a
scholar's love of research. Much like the objects that we
bestow with meaning, this book carries a rich, lingering
resonance. A gem."

— Andrew McCarthy, actor, director, and
author of *The Longest Way Home* (2013)

A treasure trove of … fascinating deep dives into
the history of travel keepsakes … Potts walks us
through the origins of some of the most popular
vacation memorabilia, including postcards and the
still confoundedly ubiquitous souvenir spoons. He
also examines the history of the more somber side
of mementos, those depicting crimes and tragedies.
Overall, the book, as do souvenirs themselves, speaks
to the broader issues of time, memory, adventure, and
nostalgia."

— *The Boston Globe*

Veil

" Slim but formidable."

—*London Review of Books*

" Rafia Zakaria's Veil shifts the balance away from white secular Europe toward the experience of Muslim women, mapping the stereotypical representations of the veil in Western culture and then reflecting, in an intensely personal way, on the many meanings that the veil can have for the people who wear it . . . [*Veil* is] useful and important, providing needed insight and detail to deepen our understanding of how we got here—a necessary step for thinking about whether and how we might be able to move to a better place."

—*The Nation*

" An intellectually bracing, beautifully written exploration of an item of clothing all too freighted with meaning."

—Molly Crabapple, artist, journalist, and author of *Drawing Blood (2015)*